THE PASSION OF PERPETUA

A Latin Text of the

Passio Sanctarum Perpetuae et Felicitatis

with Running Vocabulary and Commentary

THE **EXPERRECTA** SERIES

Women Latin Authors

Volume 1: The Passion of Perpetua

Series Editors:

Thomas G. Hendrickson
John T. Lanier
Anna C. Pisarello

pixeliapublishing.org

THE PASSION OF PERPETUA

A Latin Text of the

Passio Sanctarum Perpetuae et Felicitatis

with Running Vocabulary and Commentary

Mia Donato
Carolyn Engargiola
Eli Gendreau-Distler
Elizabeth Hasapis
Thomas G. Hendrickson
Jacob Nguyen
Siddharth Pant
Shamika Podila
Anna Riordan
Oliver Thompson

PIXELIA PUBLISHING

The Passion of Perpetua: A Latin Text of the *Passio Sanctarum Perpetuae et Felicitatis* with Running Vocabulary and Commentary

First Edition

ISBN: 978-1-7370330-0-4

Published by Pixelia Publishing
pixeliapublishing.org

Cover photo by Khimish Sharma
Cover design by Arhan Surapaneni

Font: Adobe Jenson Pro

CONTENTS

ACKNOWLEDGEMENTS

We thank Stanford Online High School for providing the opportunity for the authors to produce this edition as part of an advanced Latin course. Josh Carlson, Tomohiro Hoshi, and Christine Van Winkle secured financial support for the project and helped us to overcome several serious logistical hurdles. John Lanier, Anna Pisarello, and Ben Wiebracht provided invaluable feedback and advice on the manuscript. Arhan Surapaneni (10th grade) designed our cover.

We would also like to express our gratitude to several people who provided inspiration for different aspects of this volume. Among the leaders in bringing to light Latin texts written by women, we would especially like to highlight the work of Laurie Churchill, Phyllis Brown, and Jane Jeffrey (Women Writing Latin); Joan Ferrante (epistolae.ctl.columbia.edu); Skye Shirley (skyeshirley.com); and Jane Stevenson (Women Latin Poets). Carlos Noreña provided a model for student-teacher co-publication in the humanities. Dickinson College Commentaries, Eleanor Arnold (latinteachertoolbox.com), Faenum Publishing, and Geoffrey Steadman (geoffreysteadman.com) have led the way in offering open-access editions of Greek and Latin texts for students.

We owe a special debt of gratitude to Geoffrey Steadman in particular. Steadman was among the first to grasp the possibilities of print-on-demand publishing for classical works. In addition, his preferred format (a text with running vocabulary and commentary) anticipated the current trend of prioritizing ease of comprehension so that students can benefit from reading extensively. Steadman provided us not just inspiration but material aid: the foundation of this project was a text and running vocabulary that he had created for his own publications but generously passed on for us to use.

Finally, we would like to thank the many friends and family members who helped us and supported us over the course of this last year. The global pandemic has made it a hard year for all, and we are especially grateful for the members of our various overlapping communities, whose care has allowed this project to flourish even in these difficult times.

ABOUT THE EXPERRECTA SERIES

Women have written a good deal of Latin literature, but there are very few editions of that literature geared to student use. The goal of the Experrecta series is to create student editions of Latin texts written by women. The aim of each edition is to assist students in reading the works of these authors in the original Latin. To that end, each edition will include help with the author's vocabulary and grammar, as well as an introduction to provide historical background on her life and works. Our primary focus will be those authors for whom there are no student editions available, though we will also produce editions of those few women authors whose works do exist in student editions if we feel that we can improve on those editions in some way. We have decided to start with Vibia Perpetua since she was among the first women to write a surviving Latin work. The name of the series comes from Perpetua herself. In Perpetua's narrative she recounts a series of visions, each of which ends with the phrase *Et experrēcta sum* ("And I awoke"). This series will be populated by texts that have long been slumbering and are now waking to a new dawn and a new readership in Latin classrooms.

About The Authors

Joint authorship is uncommon in the humanities. A byline with ten names might well prompt questions, so we wanted to say a few words about our methods.

This book is the culmination of a project undertaken in an advanced Latin course at Stanford Online High School in the academic year 2020–2021. Hendrickson taught the course and organized the project. Geoffrey Steadman provided the Latin text, for which he had already added macrons and drawn up a preliminary running vocabulary. (Steadman declined an authorship credit.) Hendrickson divided the text into nine sections, and each student (Donato, Engargiola, Gendreau-Distler, Hasapis, Nguyen, Pant, Podila, Riordan, and Thompson) became section editor for one section of the text. As a first stage in the project, section editors checked the macrons in their sections. The macrons had been added through a software program (alatius.com/macronizer) which was generally effective but did need corrections. As a second stage, students revised the vocabulary in their sections. As a third stage, each section editor wrote a commentary for their section, deciding what needed to be explained in the text and how to explain it. Section editors also provided peer review for each other after every stage of the project, and Hendrickson provided a final round of revisions. Hendrickson wrote the Introduction, which the students then revised in turn. Given this truly collaborative effort, a shared byline seemed the most appropriate way to describe the authorship of this edition.

INTRODUCTION

I. THE PURPOSE OF THIS EDITION

Perpetua was a young African woman who fell in with an obscure religious sect that must have seemed to outsiders like a kind of death-cult. She was arrested around the year 203 CE along with several other practitioners on unspecified charges, and it appears that her group was believed to pose a threat to the safety of the larger community. Given the opportunity to renounce the group and walk free, Perpetua chose execution in the arena.

The *Passiō*, an account of her death, includes Perpetua's prison diary, in which the already-radicalized woman describes her progressive alienation from her family. Perpetua was a prophet and a leader in her sect, and her narrative describes a series of visions: a ladder rigged with lacerating blades and tearing hooks, the torment of a family member, and a final climactic vision in which she becomes a man and fights hand-to-hand against the devil. Transgressive, radical, and determined to face down a violent death: Perpetua is a formidable figure.

Perpetua was a Christian. Her beliefs would have seemed strange and alarming to many in the high Roman empire, a fact that can be easy to forget in the modern day, given that Christianity is relatively well-known and mainstream in most English-speaking countries. We have created this edition with the hope of better understanding Perpetua in the context of her own place and time.[1]

...

The *Passiō* is an ideal text for students. One immediate advantage of the *Passiō* is the relative simplicity of the prose. Sentences are generally short and grammatically straightforward, which makes it easier for students to read substantial portions and thereby build their familiarity with the Latin language. Indeed, one of our

---

[1] We do not mean to suggest that we are the first to see how radical Perpetua was in her own context (on which, see e.g., Gold 2018, Cooper 2011, and Shaw 1993). Rather, we mean to bring this aspect of her character, well known to the scholarly world, to a student audience.

guiding pedagogical principles is that student time is spent more effectively reading and comprehending Latin than it is flipping through a dictionary or a grammar book.[2] As such, we offer vocabulary and grammatical help directly on each page.

The *Passiō* is also an ideal text for students because Perpetua's voice makes a distinct contribution to the canon of Latin authors. Perpetua was almost certainly from a wealthy background,[3] but as an African woman and a member of a then-minority religion, she presents us with a different perspective from the ones we usually see in ancient Latin texts. Her narrative is among the earliest pieces of Latin prose written by a woman. It is also the perspective of a member of an unpopular religious minority, a minority that was in the process of going mainstream, but that, at least in Perpetua's time and place, involved radical practices like female leadership and a seemingly fanatical embrace of suffering and death.

Moreover, Perpetua is a useful figure for thinking about Roman culture precisely because she is a boundary-crosser. She was a woman who defied her father and defied the expectations placed on her as a daughter and a mother. She also defied the religious traditions of the mainstream community by refusing to sacrifice to the gods and the emperors. This refusal would have been seen as politically subversive and as risking real, material danger by alienating the community from the gods' goodwill. Perpetua's narrative provides an ideal jumping-off point for discussions about gender, class, religion, race, and social order in the Roman world.

This introductory chapter seeks to provide students with background information about the *Passiō*. We have tried to make each section of the introduction intelligible on its own, since students might read different sections as needed rather than the whole start-to-finish. As such, there is necessarily some occasional repetition from section to section.

---

[2] Clyde Pharr made this point in his justification for providing an on-page vocabulary for his 1930 edition of the *Aeneid*, and research on language acquisition has certainly reinforced this approach.

[3] It is worth noting, however, that Cooper (2011) argues that Perpetua came from a non-elite background (for more, see Introduction IV.A).

II. THE AUTHORSHIP OF THE *PASSIŌ*

This book is an edition of the full work in which Perpetua's narrative comes down to us, which has traditionally been called the *Passiō Sānctārum Perpetuae et Fēlīcītātis* (*The Passion*[4] *of Saints Perpetua and Felicity*).[5] This work contains, or purports to contain, the writings of three authors: Perpetua, whose narrative takes up chapters 3–10; Satyrus, one of Perpetua's companions, whose narrative is chapters 11.2–13.8; and an embedding narrative frame by an anonymous editor whom we refer to as the "Redactor" (chapters 1–2, 11.1, and 14–21). Felicity was an enslaved woman who was arrested and executed with Perpetua. She did not author any portion of the work, and her name in the title probably reflects her prominence in the narrative: she fears that her pregnancy might keep her from execution (and therefore martyrdom), and she miraculously undergoes a premature labor (ch. 15). Felicity's name in the title may also reflect the co-celebration of Perpetua and Felicity on the same feast day (March 7) in Christian communities.

The Redactor claims to have collected and presented verbatim the narrative "written by Perpetua's own hand, showing her own perspective" (ch. 2.3), and likewise Satyrus's narrative "which he himself wrote up" (ch. 11.1). Yet there is some question as to whether the Redactor might have not just collected these narratives, but edited them as well. At the very least, the Redactor added *inquit* ("she/he said") as the second word of each narrative to mark the transition to a new speaker (ch. 3.1, 11.2). There is debate as to whether the Redactor might have made other alterations to the text as well.[6]

Indeed, it has even been argued that Perpetua never existed, and that the Redactor composed her narrative. A frequently cited reason for doubt is that conditions in Roman prisons could be atrocious, which calls into question whether someone could write a lengthy narrative there.[7] Yet Perpetua might have dictated the narra-

---

[4] We translate the Latin word *passiō* here as "passion," but the word has other relevant meanings, such as "endurance" and "suffering."

[5] This title goes back to the first print edition in 1663, but a similar title is found in most of the manuscripts (see the apparatus in Heffernan 2012: 104), and it might be more useful to think of this name as a description rather than a title in the modern sense.

[6] Heffernan (1995) argues for several possible editorial insertions.

[7] Gold (2018: 15–18) surveys various arguments for and against Perpetua's authorship of her narrative.

tive to one of her many guests (ch. 9.1), and in addition she describes the prison as having better and worse places—the former being available for a bribe (ch. 3.5–8).

Other scholars have expressed some doubts about the *Passiō's* authorship without going so far as directly asserting that the Redactor must have written the whole: Perkins (2007) argues that the descriptions of childbirth and nursing in the *Passiō* seem to dramatize contemporary theological debates about whether Jesus had real, physical flesh and a real, physical birth; Adams (2016: 337–339) notes that Perpetua, Satyrus, and the Redactor share a linguistic tick in their usage of *ille / illa / illud* as an unemphatic pronoun (on this see Introduction VI.L).[8] Yet the descriptions of child-birth and nursing could be both true *and* symbolically significant; moreover, Perpetua and Satyrus likely come from the same speech community as the Redactor, making it unsurprising that they would share some linguistic features. As a final point, it seems unlikely that the Redactor wrote the entire text, given that his portrayal of Perpetua is at odds with her portrayal of herself.

The Redactor clearly tried both to capitalize on Perpetua's extraordinariness and at the same time to tone down the most radical aspects of her character, as Shaw (1993) first argued. The Redactor is deeply concerned with convincing readers that the Holy Spirit is still active in the world, and that it is bringing about visions and prophecies (see especially ch. 1 and 21). Perpetua's visions make her a compelling illustration of this belief. And yet the Redactor also attempts to present Perpetua as conforming to traditional gender expectations, such as when he writes that when her clothes were torn in the arena, she stopped to cover her thigh, "more mindful of her propriety (*pudor*) than of her pain" (ch. 20.4).[9] Whatever one can say about Perpetua, she does not seem mindful of her propriety. She argues with her father and defies his wishes (ch. 3, 5–6, 9), she undermines the wellbeing of her family (ch. 5.4), and she is even apparently ready to abandon her son to death (ch. 5.3). Indeed, she repeatedly inverts the power structure of gender hierarchies. She uses language throughout that portrays her metaphorically as a

---

[8] See also the broader analysis of the linguistic differences between the narratives at Adams 2016: 342–351.

[9] The Redactor's description of Perpetua here is especially suspect because there was a description of an identical action in a well-known play of Euripides (*Hecuba* 568–70). In the play Polyxena, a Trojan princess, covers her body in modesty while she is being killed as a human sacrifice to the ghost of Achilles.

wrestler, grappling with male authority figures and casting them down. In her final vision she even sees herself becoming a man and engaging in a wrestling match with the devil (ch. 10). It would seem strange for the Redactor to have invented Perpetua when he seems to wish she were different than she was.

III. SUMMARY OF THE *PASSIŌ*

In order to help students better navigate this introduction and the Latin text itself, we provide here a short summary of the *Passiō*.

Chapters 1–2: The Redactor's Preface

The Redactor begins by presenting the purpose of sharing this story: so that people will see that the Holy Spirit is still active in the world and still granting prophecies and visions (ch. 1). He then provides a bit of brief background information: that Perpetua was arrested along with four others, named Revocatus, Felicity, Saturninus, and Secundulus (ch. 2). All five were "catechumens," that is, students of Christianity who had not yet been formally initiated into the religion through baptism.[10]

Chapters 3–10: Perpetua's Narrative

Perpetua begins her narrative by recounting an argument she had with her father while under house arrest (ch. 3). He wants her to abandon Christianity, but she replies that she cannot be other than she is: a Christian. Perpetua and her companions are then baptized, and sometime later they are taken to prison. Perpetua has a brief visit from her mother and brother, and she decides to keep her infant son in prison with her.

When one of her fellow prisoners asks her for a prophecy about their fate, Perpetua receives a vision in her sleep: a bronze ladder to heaven, full of danger (ch. 4). The ladder has already been climbed by Satyrus, who had been teaching the catechumens and who had turned himself in after their arrest. When Perpetua climbs

---

[10] For more on the terms "catechumen" and "baptism," see Introduction V.A. For the legal status of Christianity in Perpetua's day, see Introduction V.B.

the ladder she finds a gray-haired shepherd who gives her a bite of food. She wakes up and interprets this vision as foretelling her death.

Perpetua's father then visits her in prison, again seeking to dissuade her (ch. 5). He points out the harm she will inflict on her family, both because they love her and because they will become suspect themselves. Perpetua is resolute.

Perpetua then receives her trial (ch. 6). The procurator asks Perpetua to perform a sacrifice for the health and safety of the emperors. (At the time, Septimius Severus and his son Caracalla were joint emperors). She refuses. He asks if she is a Christian. She affirms it. He condemns her to be thrown to the beasts, and her father takes away her son.

Perpetua then receives a vision of her brother Dinocrates, who had died in childhood (ch. 7). In the vision Dinocrates is being tormented in the afterlife. He thirsts and there is a pool of water, but he is unable to reach it. Perpetua prays for Dinocrates, confident that she can help him. She is also transferred to a military prison where she will fight at Games held in celebration of Geta, son of Septimius Severus and younger brother of Caracalla.

Perpetua receives another vision of Dinocrates (ch. 8). He is now refreshed, and he drinks and plays in the water.

The warden of Perpetua's military prison, Pudens, is deeply impressed by Perpetua and her companions (ch. 9). Perpetua's father visits her for a final time, grieving and in utter despair. Perpetua feels sorry for him but stands firm.

On the night before the Games, Perpetua receives a final vision, in a dream as always (ch. 10). She sees herself in the arena, preparing to fight. Her clothes are stripped off and she becomes a man. She fights against a mysterious Egyptian, over whom she is victorious. She awakes and concludes that she will be fighting against the devil.

Chapters 11–13: Satyrus's Narrative

The Redactor now introduces the narrative of Satyrus, whom Perpetua had mentioned as her teacher. Satyrus recounts a vision of the afterlife, in which angels bring him and Perpetua to a heavenly garden where they see other martyrs who had died previously (ch. 11). Angels then bring Satyrus and Perpetua before the throne of God (ch. 12). Finally, Satyrus and Perpetua encounter a bickering bishop and priest, whose dispute Perpetua mediates (ch. 13).

Chapters 14–21: The Redactor Describes the Fate of Perpetua and her Companions

The Redactor concludes the visions of Perpetua and Satyrus, then recounts some stories of their time in prison, beginning by noting the death of a martyr named Secundulus who died while incarcerated (ch. 14). The Redactor then recounts the story of Felicity, an enslaved woman who was arrested with Perpetua (ch. 15). Felicity was eight months pregnant, and she feared that her pregnancy would delay her execution. She wanted to die along with her companions, but the law did not allow pregnant women to be executed. Her fellow Christians were also saddened and they prayed for her. She then went into labor prematurely. The Redactor tells a story of Perpetua confronting their jailer over the conditions in the prison; the jailer relents (ch. 16). The Redactor also describes their last meal in prison, which they turn into a Feast of Love (ch. 17; for the term see Introduction V.A).

Finally, the Redactor narrates the day of the Games (ch. 18–21). Perpetua and her companions enter the arena; Perpetua convinces the tribune not to force them to wear costumes (ch. 18). The Redactor describes the mauling of Saturninus, Revocatus, and Satyrus, who are attacked by various animals (ch. 19). The Redactor also describes the mauling of Perpetua and Felicity, who make a final stand together (ch. 20). The Redactor ends by describing the death of Satyrus, who directed his last words to the warden Pudens, now converted to Christianity, and the Redactor describes the death of Perpetua, who grabbed a gladiator's sword and pulled it into her throat (ch. 21).

IV. PEOPLE IN THE *PASSIŌ*[11]

A. Perpetua

Perpetua had a multifaceted identity. She was (probably) from a high-status background, she was a woman with a complex gender identity, she was an African Roman, and she was a Christian. This section of the introduction will explore the evidence about Perpetua's background.

Our only knowledge about Perpetua comes from the text of the *Passiō* itself. In introducing Perpetua, the Redactor provides the following information (ch. 2.1–3):

> ...Vibia Perpetua, respectably born, liberally educated, lawfully wed, having a father and mother and two brothers, one of whom was, like her, a catechumen, and an infant son at her breasts. She was around 22 years old.

The Redactor's description has aroused some doubts. The Redactor is at pains to emphasize Perpetua's elite status, and yet there are hints that the picture does not quite add up. If she had been "respectably born," how can it be that a Roman official summarily ordered her father to be beaten, given that citizens could not receive corporal punishment without a trial? If Perpetua herself were a citizen, how could she have been sentenced to be thrown to the beasts, a method of execution usually reserved for non-citizens? If she were "lawfully wed," why is her son returned to her family rather than her husband's, as required by Roman law? And where is that husband anyway? Perpetua herself never mentions him once.

Due to questions like these, Cooper (2011) has suggested that the Redactor cannot be trusted on Perpetua's background. If she were a woman of lower status, many of these problems would be solved.

And yet, these problems might not require such a drastic conclusion. After all, the Roman official might have been overstepping his bounds in having Perpetua's father beaten, or perhaps Perpetua is exaggerating the confrontation. And it might

---

[11] For more information on the people in the *Passiō*, see Heffernan 2012: 3–59.

have been the case that Perpetua had been offered a different form of execution but preferred to be thrown to the beasts, which would both keep her with her fellow Christians (clearly a priority, see ch. 15.2–3) and offer her a public demonstration of her resolve. It also weighs in favor of her elite status that she was clearly "liberally educated," given that she spoke Greek (ch. 13.4), made allusions to Plato (ch. 3.1–2), and authored her own narrative. This is not to say that the Redactor is necessarily to be believed in claiming elite status for Perpetua; rather, it is simply the more likely option, though the conclusion is not without its problems.

Whatever her class status, Perpetua was clearly in a position of leadership among her fellow Christians. She was a prophet, and when one of her companions in jail asks her to foretell whether they will be killed or released (ch. 4.1), Perpetua responds that she speaks with the Lord and that she has no doubt she can receive a vision to learn the future (ch. 4.2); her prayers can evidently release someone from suffering in the afterlife (ch. 7–8); Satyrus depicts Perpetua as mediating a dispute between a priest and a bishop in his vision (ch. 13.1–4); and the Redactor describes Perpetua speaking on behalf of her companions in disputes with state officials (ch. 16.2–4, 18.4–6).

In addition to her leadership, one of Perpetua's most striking characteristics is her resolve. Perpetua's father and Hilarianus the procurator both urge her to desist from her path and to consider the pain and hardship she will inflict on her loving family (ch. 5–6). She grieves for their pain, but she does not for a moment flinch in her determination. Indeed, Perpetua and her companions joyfully embrace suffering and death. When sentenced to be thrown to the beasts, a death that is terrifying, painful, and humiliating, Perpetua reports that she and her companions were in cheerful high-spirits (*hilarēs*, ch. 6.6). The Redactor likewise describes them as rejoicing when they learn that they will be brutally scourged before their execution (ch. 18.9). Yet Perpetua stands apart from the rest. She is so fierce that when a novice gladiator's hand trembles as he tries to kill her, she grabs the sword herself and pulls it into her throat. "Perhaps such a woman could not have been killed otherwise," concludes the Redactor (ch. 21.10), "than if she herself had willed it."

Perpetua's leadership and resolve are all the more unusual for the time because they defied gender-based expectations.[12] Indeed, given that Romans saw strength and power as masculine characteristics, a woman who was strong and powerful would be seen as acting male, and might see herself as such. In that sense, Perpetua is gender non-conforming even apart from her final vision, in which she becomes male even while remaining female (*facta sum masculus*, ch. 10.7).[13] Perpetua is not unique here; there is a larger phenomenon of women in the early Christian world being said to "become male," a notion that could entail the rejection of a range of expected female characteristics or behaviors in favor of male characteristics and behaviors.[14] "Becoming male" might sometimes be a source of criticism, as a transgression of boundaries, but it might also be a source of praise, as transcending a state deemed to be inferior (that is, being a woman). To be clear, Perpetua sees herself as a woman throughout the narrative, and she foregrounds her motherhood and nursing. That said, it is also clear that she presents some of her actions and traits as masculine, and clear that some contemporaries were bothered by this violation of gender norms.

Perpetua was an African Roman, and modern students might well wonder whether she was Black. The question is a complex one. First, it is worth noting that there is a risk of anachronism in using modern racial categories to describe ancient people, and skin-color was not a primary marker of race in the ancient Mediterranean. Yet if we look at race as a social construction rather than a biological fact, the study of racial formation can shed critical light on the history of the ancient Mediterranean, as McCoskey (2012) and others have shown. A second reason for caution is that even in the modern world the term "Black" does not have fixed and absolute boundaries, and the term sometimes includes and sometimes excludes the Berber and Semitic peoples of North Africa. For our part, we do not feel that it is

---

[12] For more detail on Perpetua and gender, see Gold 2018: 23–46.

[13] This gender non-conformity, it should be noted, is distinct from sexual orientation, although some have speculated about the relationship between Perpetua and Felicity, largely on the basis of the absent husbands and on Perpetua and Felicity standing together in the face of death. Boswell (1994: 139–161), for instance, suggests that they might have been perceived as a couple in early Christian communities, and in the modern day the two have been embraced by many in the LGBTQ Christian community.

[14] For more on the rhetoric of "becoming male" in early Christian texts, see Gold 2018: 37–39.

our place to claim Perpetua as Black (nor to deny it).[15] A further complication is that it is not clear whether Perpetua was descended from North Africa's Punic inhabitants, from Roman colonists, or from both. Her name is Latin, but the name tells us nothing about her ancestry. As the province of Africa increasingly adopted and adapted Roman customs, there were many examples of individuals having both a Punic and Latin version of their name, and we can even see evidence of families that changed their names from Punic to Latin over the course of a few generations.[16]

Finally, Perpetua was a Christian.[17] It is the only part of her identity that she explicitly comments on, and she considers it an unalterable part of her being. When her father tries to persuade her to leave jail and abandon her Christianity, she points across the room at a pitcher. "Can that pitcher be called by any other name than what it is?" she asks, "In the same way I can't call myself something other than what I am, a Christian" (ch. 3.2). It is this part of her identity that Perpetua sees as most important, and it is what drives her defiance of authority figures, her abandonment of her family, her endurance, and her resolve to undergo a brutal death.

B. Perpetua's Biological Family

Over the course of Perpetua's narrative, she becomes increasingly alienated from the living members of her biological family as she embraces her identity in her new spiritual family.

Perpetua's father is her chief antagonist through most of her narrative (ch. 3–9). At times angry, at times grief-stricken, he tries to dissuade Perpetua from her resolution to suffer and die. Her father represents the traditional values of the mainstream community: that she should obey him, that she should care for her child, and that she should be concerned about how her actions will affect their wider family. Perpetua not only defies these values, she depicts herself as triumph-

---

[15] We do note that several Black Catholic groups embrace Perpetua as part of their heritage.

[16] Adams (2003: 213–224) analyzes the inscriptional evidence for Latin and Punic nomenclature.

[17] For more background on early Christianity, see Introduction V.

ing over them. The familial and gender power-structure is inverted: his threats are empty and his pleas do not sway her, even as he supplicates her and ultimately calls her "master" (ch. 5.5).

Perpetua's mother and one of her brothers visit her in prison, and she briefly entrusts her son to them (ch. 3.8). Perpetua also had a deceased brother, Dinocrates, who is the only family member whom she refers to by name. Dinocrates had died in childhood from a tumor (ch. 7.5). In a vision she sees him suffering in the afterlife, thirsting but unable to drink (ch. 7.4–8). She and her fellow prisoners pray for Dinocrates, and she receives another vision of him happy and refreshed: he has been released from torment (ch. 8).

Perpetua had a son who was young enough to be nursing. The son was with her in prison when she was first incarcerated (ch. 3.8–9), but her father took him away once she had been tried and convicted (ch. 6.6–7). Her father's action has aroused some debate, since under Roman law the child should go to her husband; or, if her husband were dead, to his family.

Perpetua's son brings up the question of the absent husband. The Redactor refers to Perpetua as "lawfully wed" (ch. 2.1), yet there is no mention of Perpetua's husband anywhere in her narrative. Various theories have been advanced as to his identity. Perhaps he had died. Perhaps he had abandoned her, or she him, whether before or after she took up Christianity. Perhaps she was not married after all, but rather a concubine (Cooper 2011). Perhaps her husband was in fact Satyrus, whose narrative follows hers in the text (Osiek 2002). In the end, whatever her marital circumstances, Perpetua herself did not find them relevant to telling her story.

As for the family's background, the Redactor characterizes it as high status, and Perpetua was clearly well educated. She claims that all her relations apart from her father will rejoice in her suffering (ch. 5.6), which suggests that they might be Christian, even apart from the one brother that the Redactor specifically names as a catechumen. Even so, Perpetua's remark about their joy might be an exaggeration: she elsewhere writes that her mother and one brother visited her in prison and grieved for her circumstances (ch. 3.8). Perpetua repeatedly emphasizes her sympathy for her family members and her consciousness of the pain they feel for her (regarding her mother and brother at ch. 3.8, her son at 3.9, and her father at

5.6, 6.5, and 9.3). Yet she expresses no hesitation or doubts about her course of action, and no diminishment of the joy she expresses at the prospect of her suffering and death.

C. Perpetua's Religious Family

The authors of the *Passiō* saw their fellow Christians as members of a spiritual family. They referred to each other as "brother" (*frāter*, ch. 1.6, 13.8), "sister" (*soror*, ch. 15.7), "papa" (*papa*, ch. 13.3) and "dear little sons" (*filiolī*, ch. 1.6). Indeed, there are cases where it is not clear whether a "brother" in question is Perpetua's biological brother or spiritual brother (ch. 4.1, 16.4, 20.10).

The Redactor writes that Perpetua was arrested with four other catechumens: Revocatus, Felicity, Saturninus, and Secundulus (ch. 2.1). The Redactor refers to Felicity as the "fellow slave" (*conserva*) of Revocatus, which provides an indication of their status. It is possible that Saturninus and Secundulus were freedmen, given that they are each referred to by a single name, but this status is not certain. We only get a few details about the male catechumens, mostly the details of their deaths (ch. 18–21), but the Redactor spends a significant amount of space on Felicity.

The Redactor writes that Felicity was pregnant when arrested, and that she feared that her pregnancy would keep her from being executed with her comrades (ch. 15.2). He writes that she was saved from this fate by the prayers of her fellow Christians, which were able to miraculously bring about a difficult, premature labor (ch. 15.4–5). As with Perpetua, the father of her child is not mentioned. And as with Perpetua, there is a seeming illegality with the child's fate: Felicity gives the child, a daughter, to a fellow Christian to raise (ch. 15.7), though legally the child would belong to whoever was holding Felicity in slavery.

Perhaps the most significant member of Perpetua's religious family is Satyrus, the man who had been a teacher to Perpetua and the other catechumens and had turned himself in once they were arrested (ch. 4.5). Perpetua sees him as a companion in her first vision (ch. 4), and his own vision makes up chapters 11–13. His death and final words take up a prominent place in the Redactor's description of what happened at the Games (ch. 19–21).

13

A handful of other co-religionists make minor appearances in the narrative: the deacons Pomponius and Tertius (ch. 3.7, 6.7, 10.1), a man who asks Perpetua to foretell the future (ch. 4.1), the woman who raises Felicity's daughter (ch. 15.7), various other martyrs (ch. 11.9, 14.2), a feuding bishop and priest (ch. 13.1–5), and a catechumen named Rusticus who was particularly attached to Perpetua (ch. 20.8).

D. Government Officials

Three named figures are part of the machinery of the Roman state. Several other figures are unnamed: prison guards who cajole and mock (ch. 3.6, 15.5), as well as a tribune in charge of the prison (ch. 16.2–4) and the gladiatorial games (ch. 18.6).

The most significant named figures are Hilarianus, a procurator, and Pudens, the warden of Perpetua's prison. The procurator Hilarianus oversaw Perpetua's trial and conviction (ch. 6), and he was also present at her execution (ch. 18.8). Hilarianus seems to have been of equestrian rank, and his position was a relatively senior one among lower-level officials. Hilarianus would not normally have had the authority to carry out executions, but he had taken over for the third named official, a deceased proconsul, who is identified as Minucius Timianus in the Latin manuscripts of the *Passiō* and Minucius Oppimianus in the Greek translation. Oppimianus is more likely correct, since we have other evidence of a proconsul of Africa named Oppimianus who died in early 203 CE, which also provides the best evidence for Perpetua's date.

Pudens, on the other hand, was a relatively lower-ranking soldier known as an *optiō*: basically a centurion's assistant. Pudens was in charge of the military prison holding Perpetua and her fellow companions, who apparently impressed him greatly (ch. 9.1). The Redactor writes that he later converted to Christianity at some point while overseeing their incarceration (ch. 16.4), and Satyrus addresses Pudens with his last words and gives him a bloody ring as a remembrance (ch. 21.1–5).

E. The Redactor

The identity of the Redactor is unknown. Robinson (1891: 47–58) argued that the Redactor should be identified as Tertullian, a Christian author from North

Africa who lived in the late-second and early-third centuries. The Redactor does share some of Tertullian's views, but that does not mean that we can identify the Redactor as Tertullian, since any number of people might have held similar views. The Redactor is particularly concerned to show that the Holy Spirit is still active in the world, just as it was in the days of the scriptures (ch. 1.1–2, 21.11). Indeed, from the Redactor's perspective, it is a false division to separate our own days from those of the scriptures, since the Holy Spirit should be, if anything, more active as the end times draw near (ch. 1.3). This was a belief shared by those in the New Prophecy movement, which was later called Montanism.

The Redactor was presumably a member of Perpetua's community. He suggests that he, and many in the community, were present for the events of the narrative (ch. 1.6), which would have taken place around 203 CE. Whether or not we trust the Redactor, it does seem likely that he was a contemporary of Perpetua, or at least that he did not live long after her, since the *Passiō* has several linguistic features that suggest that the whole was written in the third century, rather than the fourth or fifth (Adams 2016: 317).

V. PERPETUA'S RELIGION

A. Early Christian Beliefs, Books, Rituals, and Organization

This section offers some background on early Christianity that will be helpful for understanding the *Passiō*. The first goal of this section is to familiarize students with Christianity, in particular early Christian beliefs, texts, rituals, and organization. This information is especially important for students with a limited knowledge of Christianity in general. The second goal of this section is to *defamiliarize* students with Christianity. That is, students who are already familiar with Christianity are in danger of missing how strange, and alarming, all of this would have seemed in the Roman world.

Early in the first century, a Jewish prophet from humble beginnings started to make a splash in Galilee. His teachings were evidently deemed a threat to social order, and he was executed sometime around 30 CE. Soon a figure named Saul, also known as Paul, started spreading the message beyond the Jewish community, particularly in urban areas of the Greek-speaking world.

We have scant contemporary evidence for the beliefs and practices of Jesus and his followers—indeed, none from Jesus's own lifetime. The earliest evidence comes from letters written by Paul (c. 30s–50s CE), which show a conviction that Jesus was the son of the Jewish God Yahweh, that he had come back to life shortly after his execution, and that he could offer eternal life to his followers. These letters likewise suggest that the end of the world was imminent, though none could know exactly how imminent. Another set of documents, written in the following generation (c. 70–120 CE), provide accounts of Jesus's life which likewise emphasize that he was able to return to life after a gruesome execution; the four earliest of these are now called the gospels of Mark, Matthew, Luke, and John. Other documents date to a period not long after the gospels. These include the *Apocalypse of John* and the *Shepherd of Hermas*, which recount fantastical visions. Another document that dates to roughly the same era is the *Didache* (Grk. *Teaching*), which describes some of the early organization for the movement and early rituals.

These early Christian documents provide important context for understanding the *Passiō*. All of these documents were written in Greek, and there likewise existed a Greek translation of the books of the Hebrew Bible. Perpetua spoke Greek, but Latin translations would also have been available to her. These translations are now called the Old Latin versions, to differentiate them from the Vulgate version created by Jerome in the fourth century. Not all of these documents are still considered to be a part of the Christian Bible: *The Shepherd of Hermas*, for instance, is no longer considered scripture, though it seems to have had a strong influence on Perpetua.[18] There is further significance to the fluidity of the biblical canon at this period because the Redactor seems to claim that the *Passiō* should be on equal footing with sacred scriptures (ch. 1), and the rhetorical style of Perpetua and Satyrus mimics biblical narrative.[19] So the authors of the *Passiō* may have seen themselves as, in a sense, adding a book to the Bible.

These various early Christian texts mention three rituals that the *Passiō* refers to:

---

[18] Robinson (1891: 26–36) points out some parallels between *The Shepherd of Hermas* and the visions of Perpetua and Satyrus.

[19] Adams details the rhetorical and linguistic similarities between the Old Latin versions of the Bible and the narratives of Perpetua and Satyrus in his commentary on the *Passiō* (2016: 317–353); Adams suggests that there is significant "biblical pastiche" (351) in Perpetua's Latin.

1) *Immersion* (Grk. *baptisma*) was a ritual bath taken by adherents to mark their official induction into the group.[20] The Redactor describes Perpetua's companions, Satyrus and Felicity, as receiving a "second immersion" when they are drenched in blood at their execution (ch. 18.3, 21.2). There, the Redactor is using the ritual to mark an important turning point, as they are essentially now being initiated into their new rebirth in the afterlife.

2) The *Love Feast* (Grk. *agapè*) was a communal meal that was associated with the ritual *Thanksgiving* (Grk. *eucharistos*). This meal paradoxically recreates the last meal eaten by Jesus, and at the same time enacts a ritual in which participants eat the flesh and drink the blood of Jesus. It is a ritual of fellowship among the believers, and of communion with the divine. Perpetua herself alludes to this practice in her first vision, in which a heavenly shepherd shares with her a bite of food (ch. 4.9). The Redactor refers explicitly to the *Love Feast*, which he says that Perpetua and her companions shared as their own last supper before their execution (ch. 17.1). The *Love Feasts* gave rise to malicious rumors about Christians. These meals were held in private houses, and the secrecy caused suspicions in the larger community: several early Christians report that these rumors accused them of incest and cannibalism.

3) The *Kiss of Peace* was used as a greeting and also had a role in the *Love Feast*. It is a mark of recognition and fellowship among believers. Perpetua describes receiving such a kiss from a heavenly figure in a vision (ch. 10.13), and the Redactor writes that Perpetua and her companions shared such kisses as a final act before their deaths (ch. 21.7).

These documents also mention various positions within the movement, several of which appear in the *Passió*. The movement itself is called the "Assembly" (Grk. *ecclēsia*, ch. 1.5, 21.11), a word now usually translated as "Church." In this Assembly there are "supervisors" (Grk. *episcopoi*), "elders" (Grk. *presbyteres*), "assistants" (Grk. *diaconoi*), and "students" (Grk. *catechoumenoi*)— these offices are

---

[20] English-speakers refer to this practice as "baptism," simply anglicizing the Greek word. We use the term "immersion" here to keep the active meaning that it would still have had for a Greek-speaker like Perpetua.

also translated as "bishops," "priests," "deacons," and "catechumens."[21] The supervisors and elders are leadership positions, and Satyrus's narrative describes a dispute between one particular supervisor, Optatus, and an elder, Aspasius (ch. 13.1–6). "Assistants" come up occasionally in the narrative, and one assistant in particular, Pomponius, frequently comes to the aid of Perpetua and her companions once they are imprisoned. Finally, "students" (catechumens) are those who are learning the tenets of the religion but have not yet been formally inducted by the rite of immersion. Perpetua and her companions (Felicity, Revocatus, Saturninus, and Secundulus) are students at the start of the narrative when they are arrested (ch. 2.1), and they receive their immersion during a period of house-arrest before they are imprisoned (ch. 3.5). Their teacher is Satyrus, who turns himself in after they are arrested (ch. 4.5). Another student, Rusticus, is described as being particularly attached to Perpetua, and is in the arena with her (ch. 20.8–10).

These documents provide information about one other aspect of early Christianity that is crucial to understanding the narrative: Christians worshipped their God exclusively and refused to participate in sacrifices or rituals for any other gods. This refusal contributed to the group's deep unpopularity. In the Roman world, it was expected for all community members to sacrifice to the gods. The gods had an impact on just about every aspect of life, and the goodwill of the gods was necessary for peace and prosperity. Slighting the gods could result in bad harvests, natural disasters, civil unrest, or foreign invasion. A refusal to sacrifice to the gods suggested ill-will to one's community, ill-will that could result in real, material harm, and even lives lost.

B. The Legal Status of Early Christianity

The legal status of Christians in Perpetua's day was hazy. There was no specific law against Christianity in the early third century, nor was there any universal law requiring sacrifice,[22] which would have the result of de facto criminalizing Christianity. At the same time, Christians had a bad reputation, and there seems to have

---

[21] In this section we favor the more direct translations of those positions that are now ecclesiastical offices (bishop, priest, deacon), since the latter terms bring associations that probably misrepresent what they would have meant to Christians in late-second and early-third century Africa.

[22] A legal requirement to offer sacrifice was instituted only later, in 249 CE, under the emperor Decius.

been an assumption that anyone in the group was likely involved in malicious acts. A perplexed Roman governor, Pliny the Younger, wrote in 112 CE to the emperor Trajan for advice when he found Christians in his courtroom: among his questions was whether they should be punished simply for membership in the group, or only for the specific bad-acts that they (surely) were involved in (Plin. *Epistles* 10.96.2). In Pliny's case the point proved moot because he found the Christians so recalcitrant that he punished them simply for their defiance. He asked the accused if they were Christians. He had heard that Christians would be unwilling to sacrifice, and so he made it his litmus-test. He ordered them to sacrifice: those who did could go free, while those who did not would be punished for disobeying a Roman magistrate. Defiance of a magistrate was a defiance of imperial authority.

Hilarianus, the magistrate conducting Perpetua's trial, followed the same procedure as Pliny. He commanded her to make a sacrifice to the safety of the emperors: she refused (ch. 6.3–4). He asked if she were a Christian: she assented (ch. 6.4). He convicted and sentenced her (ch. 6.6).

VI. THE LATIN OF THE *PASSIŌ*

The Latin of the *Passiō* is relatively straightforward and simple, which makes it ideal for students. Yet there are several minor features that will differ from what students might expect based on what they will have learned in most textbooks, so we highlight these non-standard features here.[23]

The *Passiō* was written in the early third century. In the history of the Latin language, this date falls after, though not long after, the period called "Classical Latin," which is usually considered to be roughly 100 BCE to 100 CE. Some of the features of the *Passiō* that differ from what students will have learned in textbooks could be called "post-classical," in that they only start to be attested from the third century or later. Other non-standard features of the *Passiō* are attested in Classical Latin, but seem to be informal and so rarely appear in the high literature that most textbooks are based on. Still other features seem to be influenced by contact with the Greek language, and others show the influence of the Old Latin versions

---

[23] For more details on all these features, see the linguistic commentary on Perpetua in Adams (2016: 317–353).

of the Bible (see Introduction V.A). These various categories can overlap. For instance, the word order subject-verb-object is characteristic of informal speech, of post-classical Latin, and of the Old Latin versions of the Bible. Because of this overlap, it would not be possible to divide each of these non-standard features into discrete categories, so we present them together in a single list.

As a final point, this list is not meant to suggest that the Latin of the *Passiō* is particularly strange. Most of the features on this list are found in classical authors as well, though they tend to be less common there and so are typically avoided in textbooks.

A. Ablative of Extent of Time

Though most textbooks teach that duration of time is expressed with an accusative, the ablative can also be used, as when Perpetua writes that she gave thanks when her father was gone "for a few days" (*paucīs diēbus*, 3.4). This usage is more common in post-classical Latin, but it goes back to the classical period and can be seen in (e.g.) Cicero (*Dē Ōrāt.* 3.138) and Caesar (*BC* 1.46).[24]

B. *In* + Abl. to Express Motion Towards

Most Latin textbooks teach that the preposition *in* governs an accusative when it indicates motion towards ("into," "onto") and an ablative when it indicates static location ("in," "on"). In the *Passiō*, however, this distinction has started to break down, as when Perpetua writes that she went "into the middle of the arena" (*in mediā arēnā*, 10.4) or was lifted "into the air" (*in āere*, 10.11). The Redactor likewise uses this construction, writing about Perpetua and others going "into the middle" (*in mediō*, 21.7) of the arena, and writing about when the sword went "into their body" (*in eōrum corpore*, 21.7). This usage appears in pre-classical literature as well as in post-classical literature.[25]

---

[24] For more on the ablative of extent of time, see Pinkster (2015: 845–846).

[25] For more on the phenomenon of "*in* + abl." indicating motion towards, see Adams (2016: 327).

C. Ablative of Means with the Preposition *Dē*

In post-classical Latin, the preposition *dē* came to be used with the ablative in a wider range of uses than it had in the classical period. The *Passiō* sometimes uses *dē*, for instance, with the ablative of means, as when Dinocrates plays "with water" (*dē aquā*, 8.4). This usage becomes common in literary prose in the sixth century, but it occurs earlier in informal Latin and in the Old Latin versions of the Bible (Adams 2013: 302–303).

D. Verbs Governing Unusual Cases

There are a few cases in the *Passiō* in which a verb governs a different case than it would in Classical Latin. The verb *carēre* ("to lack") takes an accusative object rather than an ablative (3.4); the verb *nocēre* ("to hurt") takes an accusative object rather than a dative (ch. 4.6); and the deponent verb *miserērī* ("to pity") takes a dative rather than a genitive (ch. 5.2, 6.2).

E. Pluperfect Subjunctive Functioning as an Imperfect Subjunctive

In later Latin, the pluperfect subjunctive comes to be used in place of the imperfect subjunctive. Indeed, the imperfect subjunctive in most modern romance languages clearly shows its origins as a Latin pluperfect (e.g. French *je parlasse*, Italian *io parlassi*). In the *Passiō* the pluperfect subjunctive occasionally functions as an imperfect, as when Perpetua writes "I was without my father" (*caruissem patrem*, 3.4).

F. Perfect rather than Imperfect Stem in Compound Verb Forms

In passive verb forms, the *Passiō* sometimes uses forms of "to be" using the perfect stem rather than the imperfect stem, as when Perpetua's father says "you will have suffered" (*fueris passa*, 5.4) rather than *eris passa* for the future perfect. The same phenomenon occurs when the Redactor writes that Felicity "had been arrested" (*fuerat apprehēnsa*, 15.2) rather than *erat apprehēnsa* in the pluperfect. There is

no real difference in meaning between these forms. Rather, they are alternate forms that start in the classical period and gradually become more common.[26]

G. Subjunctive in *Quod*-Clauses

Perpetua tends to use the subjunctive in quod-clauses where we would normally expect the indicative (ch. 5.6, 7.1, 10.5, 18.9, and perhaps 3.4 and 7.8). There is no clear reason for the subjunctive in these cases, but the usage becomes common in post-classical Latin.[27]

H. Non-Standard Vocabulary

The *Passiō* contains some words that are non-classical and some that are classical but informal. The verbs *mandūcāre/commandūcāre* ("eat," 4.9–10), *bāsiāre* ("kiss," 5.5), and *improperāre* ("curse," 9.2) are all classical but relatively informal. Among post-classical words, the verb *cōnfortāre*, for instance, is used by Perpetua (5.6) but is otherwise not commonly attested until the fourth century. The deponent verb *fābulārī* occurs in the *Passiō* (4.2) with a sense of "to speak," which is otherwise found only in Plautus and in post-classical Latin, ultimately becoming *falar* in Portuguese and *hablar* in Spanish (after the change of word-initial f- > h-). The verb *dictāre* is technically frequentative ("to say repeatedly"), but Perpetua uses it with the simple sense of "to speak" (3.5). The Redactor uses the comparative *novītiōra* ("newer," 1.3) and *novissimiōra* (1.3), both of which are post-classical in both form and meaning. In *novītiōra*, we see that the word *novīcius* ("newly bought") came to replace *novus* ("new"), and the spelling <-ci> came to be replaced with <-ti>. In *novissimiōra*, the comparative ending -ior has been redundantly added to the superlative -issimus. Finally, Perpetua treats the verb *cupere* as if it were fourth conjugation when she uses it in the imperfect subjunctive (*cupīret*, 3.1). This form is non-standard, but it does appear in one classical author (Lucretius *Dē Rērum Nātūrā* 1.71).

The *Passiō* also contains some turns of phrase that, while not strictly non-standard, are less common and worth noting for students. The verb *introīre*, for

---

[26] For more on forms of the perfect stem in compound verbs, see Pinkster (2015: 473–476).

[27] For more on the unmotivated subjunctive in quod-clauses, see Adams (2016: 328–329).

instance, is strongly preferred to *intrāre* ("to go in"), and the adjective *ūniversī* is preferred to *omnēs* ("all"). Finally, *invicem* is regularly used in place of a reflexive pronoun.

I. Repetition of *et*

Sentences and clauses are constantly joined with *et* rather than with more complex coordinating or subordinating conjunctions, in particular in the narratives of Perpetua (ch. 3–10) and Satyrus (ch. 11–13). This stylistic feature is common in informal usage, but it is also characteristic of biblical narrative and of the Latin translations of the Bible in particular.[28]

J. Greek Words and Forms

Some Greek words in the *Passiō* come from a specifically Christian milieu: *prophētīā/prophētāre* (ch. 1.4–5 and elsewhere), *ecclēsia* (1.5 and elsewhere), *catēchūmenus* (throughout), *martyr/martyrium* (throughout), *diabolus* (3.3), *tegnon* (4.9), *horōma* (10.1), *angelus* (ch. 11–13), *agios* (12.2), *presbyter* (13.1), *episcopus* (13.1), and *ekstasis* (20.8).[29] Apart from words related to the world of Christianity, Perpetua uses the words *diastēma* ("chasm," 7.6), *fiala* ("cup," 8.3), *afa* ("sand," 10.7), *agōn* ("contest," 10.7), and the name of Perpetua's brother, *Dīnocratēs.* Perpetua and the Redactor sometimes use the Greek form of the accusative (*Dīnocratēn* at 7.1, *agapēn* at 17.1).[30] Other Greek words had diffused into Perpetua's cultural world in an indirect form: *catasta* ("platform," 6.2 and elsewhere) is ultimately from Greek *katastasis* ("establishment") and *cataractāriōrus* ("prison guard," 15.5) from Greek *katarrēktēs* ("waterfall," "portcullis").

K. Subject-Verb-Object Word Order

The most typical word order for the formal prose of Classical Latin is subject-object-verb, which is the order favored by the Redactor. Both Perpetua and Saty-

---

[28] For details on the use of paratactic *et* in the *Passiō*, see Adams (2016: 323–324).

[29] On the specifically Christian meanings of these words, see Introduction V.A.

[30] Some manuscripts of the *Passiō* end these words with the Latin accusative ending -em rather than the Greek -ēn, and the two are equally plausible.

rus tend to favor a subject-verb-object word order, which is more common in informal Latin and in post-classical Latin, as well as in the Old Latin versions of the Bible.[31]

L. *Ille / illa / illud* as an Unemphatic Pronoun (he/she/it)

The *Passiō* frequently uses *ille / illa / illud* as an unemphatic pronoun (he/she/it) rather than as a demonstrative (that/those). Frequently, this unemphatic usage comes when the word occurs after a form of *is / ea / id*, as when Satyrus writes "while we speak with them, the angels said to them" (*dum loquimur cum eīs, dīxērunt illīs angelī,* 13.5). This usage occurs from the early empire onwards.[32]

M. Dialectical Features of African Latin

Native speakers of Latin, both inside and outside of Africa, saw African Latin as a recognizably distinct way of speaking, and there were probably multiple dialects of Latin in Africa at different times and places, and among different social groups.[33] There are no uniquely African features identifiable in the *Passiō*, yet this fact is not too surprising. The regional dialects of Latin seem to have differed more in pronunciation and vocabulary rather than in morphology and syntax. As a result, these differences will not necessarily be apparent in literary texts like the *Passiō*, which generally make use of standardized spelling and a relatively standardized vocabulary.

VII. THE TEXT OF THIS EDITION

It has been a long journey for the words of the *Passiō* to travel from Perpetua's stylus to the pages of this edition. In this section we will provide some background on that journey and an explanation of how it affects what students will read here.

---

[31] For more detail on word order in the *Passiō*, see Adams (2016: 320–322 and 341–346); Adam suggests that Perpetua and Satyrus might be imitating biblical narrative.

[32] For more detail on the use of *ille / illa / illud* as an unemphatic pronoun in the *Passiō*, see Adams (2016: 337–339).

[33] Adams (2007: 516–576) outlines and analyzes the evidence for the regional features of African Latin.

Perpetua and Satyrus probably wrote or dictated their narratives while incarcerated, sometime around 203 CE. Not long afterwards the Redactor combined, and perhaps edited, these narratives— unless, of course, the Redactor himself wrote the whole *Passiō* (see Introduction II). At some later point there came into being a condensed version of the narrative, traditionally called the *Ācta Perpetuae*. A Greek translation was also made.[34] As more people wanted to read the *Passiō*, copies had to be made of the originals, and then copies of those copies, and so on. It is a difficult process to copy out an entire book, and mistakes creep into even the most careful of copies. Whatever Perpetua, Satyrus, and the Redactor wrote, the original is long gone, and so we have to reconstruct their words from the copies that survive. There are nine surviving Latin manuscripts of the full *Passiō*, and one of the Greek translation. All surviving manuscripts of the *Passiō* date from the ninth to twelfth centuries, which means that they are the product of 600–900 years of copying and recopying.

The first print edition of the *Passiō* was made by Lucas Holstenius in 1663. Since then there have been a multitude of editions, most recently the excellent critical edition of Thomas Heffernan (2012).

In this present Pixelia edition, we largely follow the text of J. Armitage Robinson (1891). We have used Robinson's edition to help keep the cost of this volume economical, since Robinson's text is the most recent critical edition in the public domain.

There are a number of places in which we depart from Robinson's text, which we list below. In two of these cases we reject emendations made by Robinson, who wanted to change the manuscript reading of *cadēbant* to *canēbant* (ch. 11.6) and *viā lātā* to *violātum* (ch. 11.8).[35] The remaining cases involve instances in which there was a problem in Robinson's primary source, the manuscript Monte Cassino

---

[34] J. Rendell Harris, who discovered the Greek translation in 1890, originally argued that the Greek version of the *Passiō* was the original and the Latin version was a translation, though he later changed his mind (Heffernan 2012: 79). Heffernan outlines why the Latin version is almost certainly the original (2012: 79–99). Shaw (2020) provides more detail on the Greek translation, its history, and its cultural context.

[35] Robinson's explanation (1891: 38–40) of these emendations will probably convince few readers.

204, which is the most complete surviving manuscript and has the fewest errors. Robinson only had access to the readings of two of the other eight surviving Latin manuscripts, and these two were not always helpful when there was a problem with the text of Monte Cassino 204.[36] As other manuscripts have been better studied, particularly in the editions of Van Beek (1936), Amat (1996), and Heffernan (2012), it has been possible to find better readings when there is an issue with Monte Cassino 204.

Textual differences between this Pixelia edition and the edition of Robinson 1891:

Robinson's Edition	Pixelia Edition
3.3 profectō	profectus
3.9 essem	esse
4.10 dulcis	dulce
5.5 mē nōn	mē iam nōn
5.6 causam	cāsum
6.5 percussit	percussus est
6.8 dēsīderat	dēsīderāvit
7.4 complūra loca erant tenebrōsa	complūrēs erant
10.2 distīnctam candidam	distīnctā candidā
10.5 datam	damnātam
10.7 dēfrigere	dēfricāre
10.8 habēns galliculās	habēns, et galliculās
10.9 et	haec
11.2 tangēbat	tangēbant
11.6 canēbant	cadēbant
11.8 violātum	viā lātā
11.9 ubi	ibi
16.1 indignē	indignī
16.2 eī respondit	eī Perpetua respondit
17.1 verba ista	verba
17.2 est, quod	est? Quid
17.2 nōbīs	vōbīs
18.2 lūcidō incessū	lūcidō vultū et placidō incessū
18.8 dē hōc	dehinc

---

[36] See Robinson's discussion of his use of manuscripts (1891: 10–15).

18.8 pervēnerint	pervēnērunt
18.9 prō ordine	per ordinem
19.3 revocātus...expertus...erat vexātus	ipse et Revocātus...expertī...vexātī sunt
19.5 post diēs	post diem
20.5 dehinc requīsīta	dehinc acū requīsīta
20.8 instupentibus	stupentibus
20.8 nesciō	nesciōquam
21.2 ēiectō	obiectus

The chapter divisions in the *Passiō* are not ancient but go back to the 1766 edition of Andrea Gallandi.[37] We have kept these chapter divisions as a matter of convenience, and for the same reason we have prefaced each chapter with a brief summary in English.

We have changed the punctuation and paragraphing from Robinson's edition, and we have added the now-standard sentence numbers to the chapter numbers. We have also changed two minor orthographic matters: we capitalize the first word of sentences and allow the assimilation of consonants in prepositional prefixes (e.g. *attonitus* rather than *adtonitus*).

We have added macrons to the Latin used throughout this edition. Since macrons are not commonly used in editions of Latin authors, especially prose authors, this decision requires a few words of explanation.

We have decided to include macrons primarily because they make the Latin easier to read by distinguishing forms that would otherwise be identical, like *puella* and *puellā*. In addition, macrons help to better represent the sounds of the Latin language, and so they are an aid to *reading* the Latin— that is, to saying or thinking the Latin words and understanding them, rather than looking at the Latin words and trying to remember their English equivalents.

While it is true that ancient Roman texts did not include macrons, it is worth noting that they likewise did not include lowercase letters and punctuation— at least

---

[37] Volume 2 of the *Bibliotheca Veterum Patrum Antiquorumque Scriptorum Ecclesiasticorum Graeco-Latina*, pp. 174–179. Venice: J. Baptistae Albrithii Hieron Fil. For more detail on this edition see Heffernan 2012: 434–435.

of the sort that modern texts employ.[38] Yet we use lowercase letters and modern punctuation because they make Latin texts easier to read, and the same rationale should apply to macrons.

VIII. A NOTE ON THE VOCABULARY AND COMMENTARY

Each page of Latin text has a running vocabulary and commentary. The vocabulary contains words that are less likely to be known by students and words that occur infrequently in the *Passiō* itself, while more common and repeated words can be found in the glossary at the back of the book. In the running vocabulary we have tried to ensure that the definition given is applicable to its use on that page. If the meaning of the word in context on the page is different from its primary definition, we place the primary definition first, followed by its meaning in context. The commentary aims primarily to help students understand the Latin, although it sometimes includes points of historical background when those serve to help make sense of the Latin. In cases where more than one interpretation of the Latin is possible, we only explain the grammar of the most likely meaning rather than exploring all possible meanings. For deeper investigation into textual and grammatical difficulties, we refer readers to the commentaries of Heffernan (2012) and Adams (2016: 317–353).

IX. FURTHER READING

There has been such a profusion of work on the *Passiō* that it would be hard to provide a bibliography of even the last ten years. All the same, we do want to point students and teachers to a few resources they might find particularly helpful.

Heffernan's critical edition (2012) provides a Latin text and English translation, along with a commentary and detailed historical and textual information. Adams (2016: 317–353) provides a linguistic commentary on chapter 10 of the *Passiō*. Gold's biography (2018) of Perpetua provides an overview of the woman, her

---

[38] Romans did employ cursive scripts, especially in informal documents, and they likewise had some punctuation marks, like the stigmē, hypostigmē, corōnis, and paragraphē, not to mention interpuncts.

world, and her legacy, as does Rea and Clarke's (2018) graphic novel. Bremmer and Formisano (2012) have gathered together a host of useful studies on a variety of aspects of the *Passiō*. Cobb (2021) offers a new study on the reception of Perpetua in late antiquity, and Cotter-Lynch (2016) on Perpetua in the middle ages.

A digital text of both the Latin and Greek versions of the *Passiō* has been made available by Open Latin and Greek,[39] and students will still find much value in Halporn's 1984 edition for the Bryn Mawr Latin Commentaries series.

---

[39] Available at https://scaife.perseus.org/library/urn:cts:greekLit:tlg2016/ (last access April 17, 2021)

BIBLIOGRAPHY

Adams, J.N. 2003. *Bilingualism and the Latin Language*. Cambridge University Press.

Adams, J.N. 2007. *The Regional Diversification of Latin, 200 BC – AD 600.* Cambridge University Press.

Adams, J.N. 2013. *Social Variation and the Latin Language*. Cambridge University Press.

Adams, J.N. 2016. *An Anthology of Informal Latin, 200 BC – AD 900.* Cambridge University Press.

Amat, Jacqueline. 1996. *Passion de Perpétue et de Félicité: suivi des Actes.* Paris: Éditions du Cerf.

Boswell, John. 1994. *Same-Sex Unions in Premodern Europe.* New York: Villard Books.

Bremmer, Jan and Marco Formisano, eds. 2012. *Perpetua's Passions.* Oxford University Press.

Cobb, L. Stephanie. 2021. *The Passion of Perpetua and Felicitas in Late Antiquity.* University of California Press.

Cooper, Kate. 2011. "A Father, A Daughter, and A Procurator: Authority and Resistance in the Prison Memoir of Perpetua of Carthage." *Gender and History* 23: 685–702.

Cotter-Lynch, Margaret. 2016. *Saint Perpetua across the Middle Ages: Mother, Gladiator, Saint.* New York: Palgrave Macmillan.

Gold, Barbara K. 2018. *Perpetua: Athlete of God.* Oxford University Press.

Halporn, James W. 1984. *Passio Sanctarum Perpetuae et Felicitatis.* Bryn Mawr Latin Commentaries.

Heffernan, Thomas. 1995. "Philology and Authorship in the *Passio Sanctarum Perpetuae et Felicitatis.*" *Traditio* 50: 315–325.

Heffernan, Thomas J. 2012. *The Passion of Perpetua and Felicity.* Oxford University Press.

McCoskey, Denise Eileen. 2012. *Race: Antiquity and its Legacy.* Oxford University Press.

Osiek, Carolyn. 2002. "Perpetua's Husband." *Journal of Early Christian Studies* 10: 287–290.

Perkins, Judith. 2007. "The Rhetoric of the Maternal Body in the *Passion of Perpetua.*" In Todd Penner and Caroline Vander Stichele, eds., *Mapping Gender in Ancient Religious Discourses*, pp. 313–332. Leiden: Brill.

Pinkster, Harm. 2015. *The Oxford Latin Syntax. Vol. I: The Simple Clause.* Oxford University Press.

Robinson, J. Armitage. 1891. *The Passion of S. Perpetua.* Cambridge University Press.

Rea, Jennifer A. (author) and Liz Clarke (illustrator). 2018. *Perpetua's Journey: Faith, Gender, and Power in the Roman Empire.* Oxford University Press.

Shaw, Brent D. 1993. "The Passion of Perpetua." *Past and Present* 139: 3–45.

Shaw, Brent D. 2020. "Doing it in Greek: Translating Perpetua." *Studies in Late Antiquity* 4: 309–345.

Van Beek, Cornelius Johannes Maria Joseph. 1936. *Passio sanctarum Perpetuae et Felicitatis.* Nijmegen: Dekker and Van de Vegt.

ABBREVIATIONS

abl.	ablative
acc.	accusative
act.	active
adj.	adjective
adv.	adverb
cf.	compare to (*cōnfer*)
ch.	chapter
comp.	comparative
conj.	conjunction
dat.	dative
e.g.	for example (*exemplī grātiā*)
fem.	feminine
fut.	future
gen.	genitive
Grk.	Greek
i.e.	that is (*id est*)
ind.	indirect
lit.	literally
masc.	masculine
neut.	neuter
nom.	nominative
pass.	passive
perf.	perfect
pl.	plural
prep.	preposition
pres.	present
sg.	singular

Passiō Sānctārum Perpetuae et Fēlīcītātis

with Running Vocabulary and Commentary

The Redactor argues that this story should be shared so that people will see that the Holy Spirit is still active in the world.

1.1 Sī vetera fideī exempla et Deī grātiam testificantia et aedificātiōnem hominis operantia proptereā in litterīs sunt dīgesta ut lēctiōne eōrum quasi repraesentātiōne rērum et Deus honōrētur et homō cōnfortētur, cūr nōn et nova documenta (aequē utrīque causae convenientia) et dīgerantur? 2. Vel quia proinde et haec vetera futūra quandōque sunt et necessāria posterīs, sī in praesentī suō tempore minōrī dēputantur auctōritātī propter praesūmptam venerātiōnem antīquitātis.

---

aedificātiō, -ōnis f.: edification; improvement
aequē: equally
antīquitās, -tātis f.: antiquity, earlier times
auctōritās, -tātis f.: authority, influence
cōnfortō (1): to strengthen
conveniō, -īre, -vēnī, -ventum: to assemble, be suitable, be convenient
dēputō (1): to consider, esteem, count as
dīgerō, -ere, -gessī, -gestum: to distribute; arrange, set in order; write down
documentum, -ī n.: example, lesson, proof
exemplum, -ī n.: example
honōrō (1): to honor, confer honor
lēctiō, -tiōnis f.: reading
littera, -ae f.: letter (alphabetic); literature (*pl.*)
minor, minus: lesser, smaller

necessārius, -a, -um: necessary
operor, -ārī, -ātus sum: to work (on), produce
posterus, -a, -um: those coming after; future generations
praesēns, -entis: present, instant
praesūmō, -ere, -sūmpsī, -sūmptum: to presume, take up
proinde: just so, even, in the same manner
proptereā: on this account, therefore
quandōque: at some time
repraesentātiō, -ōnis f.: reproduction, show, representation
testificor, -ārī, -ātus sum: to bear witness to, testify to
uterque, utraque, utrumque: either (of two)
venerātiō, -ōnis f.: reverence, veneration

Sī vetera fideī exempla … cūr nōn et nova documenta: *If old examples of faith … why not also new examples;* the Redactor is saying if the old examples were good, then why not write down new examples too, since these new ones will be good for the same reasons that the old ones were
vetera fideī exempla: *old examples of faith;* a reference to previous sacred literature
et … testificantia et … operantia: *both … testifying and … producing;* both *testificantia* and *operantia* modify *exempla*, and are the subject of *sunt dīgesta*
ut … honōrētur … cōnfortētur: purpose clause explaining why these examples should be recorded
et Deus… et homō: *both God… and man*
cūr nōn et nova … et dīgerantur: *why are not new examples too … also written down;* each *et* translates as "also" or "too" here
aequē utrīque causae convenientia: *convenientia* modifies *nova documenta;* the phrase *utrīque causae* is the indirect object of *convenientia*
Vel quia: *Because certainly;* the word *Vel* here just intensifies *quia*
et haec: *these too;* the *haec* refers to *nova documenta*
vetera: *will become old;* the predicate of *futūra … sunt*

3. Sed vīderint quī ūnam virtūtem Spīritūs ūnīus Sānctī prō aetātibus iūdicent temporum, cum maiōra reputanda sunt novītiōra, quaeque ut novissimiōra, secundum exūperātiōnem grātiae in ultima saeculī spatia dēcrētam.

4. *In novissimīs* enim *diēbus,* dīcit Dominus, *effundam dē spīritū meō super omnem carnem, et prophētābunt filiī filiaeque eōrum; et super servōs et ancillās meās dē meō spīritū effundam; et iuvenēs vīsiōnēs vidēbunt, et senēs somnia somniābunt* (Acts 2:17-18; cf. Joel 2:28-29).

---

aetās, -tātis f.: age, lifetime, time
ancilla, -ae f.: female slave, enslaved woman
dēcernō, -ere, -crēvī -crētum: to decide, judge
effundō, -ere, -fūdī, -fūsum: to pour out
exūperātiō, -ōnis f.: abundance (spelled *exūberātiō* in Classical Latin)
iūdicō (1): to decide, judge
iuvenis, -is m.: youth, young man
maior, maius: greater
novītius, -a, -um: new, recent, last

prophētō (1): to prophesy, foretell, predict
quisque, quaeque, quidque: each one, each thing
reputō (1): to count, calculate, reckon
secundum: following, in accordance with (*prep. + acc.*)
servus, -ī m.: male slave, enslaved man
somniō (1): to dream, dream of
somnium, -iī n.: dream
tempus, temporis n.: time, occasion
ultimus, -a, -um: last, final

---

vīderint: *they will figure it out;* the fut. perf. of *vidēre* can have a sense of deferment, "to attend to something later"
quī ūnam ... ūnīus ... iūdicent: *those who judge the singular power of the singular Holy Spirit; virtūs* as "power" is common in early Christian writings; the Redactor's point is that these people are wrong to believe the Holy Spirit is no longer active, since it is the *same* spirit with the *same* power in all eras
prō aetātibus ... temporum: *according to the ages of time;* this phrase goes closely with *iūdicent*
cum maiōra reputanda sunt novītiōra: *although newer things must be reckoned greater;* the sense is that not only is the Holy Spirit *still* active, but it is if anything more active, given that recent times are closer to the end times; a *cum*-clause can be concessive with the indicative, though the usage is non-standard; *novītiōra* is the subject of the pass. periphrastic, *maiōra* the predicate
novītiōra: *newer things;* two aspects of this word are non-standard: first the use of *novīcius* (originally "newly bought") for *novus* ("new"), second the spelling *novītiōra* for the comparative *novīciōra*
quaeque ut novissimiōra: *each one just as (they are) more recent;* another non-standard formation: the comparative ending *-ior* has been added to the superlative *novissimus*
exūperātiōnem grātiae ... dēcrētam: *abundance of grace ... decreed;* the Redactor wants to show that the Holy Spirit is active in granting visions, like those of Perpetua and Satyrus, because many Christians thought that the end of time was coming and that the Holy Spirit would be stronger than ever, hence the abundance of grace
in ultima saeculī spatia: *for the last spans (of time) of the world;* here *in* + acc. has a sense of "for" and *saeculum* here means "our present world," as often in early Christian writings
In novissimīs ... diēbus: *In the last days*

35

5. Itaque et nōs quī sīcut prophētīās ita et vīsiōnēs novās pariter reprōmissās et agnōscimus et honōrāmus cēterāsque virtūtēs Spīritūs Sānctī ad īnstrūmentum Ecclēsiae dēputāmus (cui et missus est īdem omnia dōnātīva administrāns in omnibus, prout ūnīcuique distribuit Dominus) necessāriō et dīgerimus et ad glōriam Deī lēctiōne celebrāmus, ut nē qua aut imbēcillitās aut dēspērātiō fideī apud veterēs tantum aestimet grātiam dīvīnitātis conversātam, sīve in martyrum sīve in revēlātiōnum dignātiōne, cum semper Deus operētur quae reprōmīsit, nōn crēdentibus in testimōnium, crēdentibus in beneficium.

---

administrō (1): to manage, regulate, direct
aestimō (1): to assess, judge
agnōscō, -ere, -nōvī, -nitum: to recognize
apud: among; at the house of (+ *acc.*)
celebrō (1): to frequent; honor, celebrate
conversō (1): to turn around; to exist along with, to be among
dēputō (1): to consider, esteem, or count as
dēspērātiō, -tiōnis f.: hopelessness
dīgerō, -ere, -gessī, -gestum: to distribute, arrange, set in order; write
dignātiō, -tiōnis f.: deeming worthy, granting
distribuō, -ere, -buī, -būtum: to distribute
dīvīnitās, -tātis f.: divinity
dōnātīvum, -ī n.: gift
Ecclēsia, -ae f.: assembly; church
honōrō (1): to honor, confer honor
imbēcillitās, -tātis f.: weakness

īnstrūmentum, -ī n.: implement, tool; instruction
lēctiō, -tiōnis f.: reading
martyr, -tyris m.: witness; martyr
necessāriō: necessarily (*adv.*)
operor, -ārī, -ātus sum: to work, produce, bring about
pariter: equally
prophētīa, -ae f.: prophecy, prediction
prout: just as, in as much as
reprōmittō, -ere, -mīsī, -missum: to promise in return
revēlātiō, -ōnis f.: an unveiling, a revelation
sīcut: just as, so as
sīve, seu: whether, or
testimōnium, -iī n.: witness, evidence
ūnusquisque, ūnaquaeque, ūnumquodque: each and every one

---

et nōs … et dīgerimus et … celebrāmus: *we too … both write and … celebrate;* the subject (*nōs*) is separated from the main verbs by a lengthy relative clause

quī … dēputāmus: *prophētīās* and *vīsiōnēs* are the direct objects of the verbs *agnōscimus et honōrāmus;* both objects are modified by the phrase *novās pariter reprōmissās;* the object of *dēputāmus* is *cēterās virtūtēs*

cui: could refer to *Ecclēsiae* or *īnstrūmentum*

īdem: refers to the Holy Spirit

ut nē qua: the *ut nē* sets up a purpose clause, though purpose clauses usually begin with just *nē;* the *qua* is a shortened version of *aliqua* ("some", "any"), as is typical before *sī, nisi, num,* and *nē*

apud veterēs tantum: *only among the ancients;* take this phrase closely with *grātiam dīvīnitātis conversātam*

nōn crēdentibus … crēdentibus: *the non-believers … the believers;* refers to the non-believers and believers in Christianity, a usage of *crēdere* that is common throughout the text

in testimōnium … in beneficium: *as a testimony … as a benefit*

6. Et nōs itaque *quod audīvimus et contrectāvimus, annūntiāmus et vōbīs,* frātrēs et fīliolī, *ut et vōs* quī interfuistis rememorēminī glōriae Dominī et quī nunc cognōscitis per audītum *commūniōnem habeātis cum* sānctīs martyribus (1 John 1.1-3), et per illōs cum dominō Iēsū Chrīstō cui est clāritās et honor in saecula saeculōrum. Āmēn.

The Redactor introduces Perpetua and those arrested with her, then informs the audience that the following narrative was written by Perpetua herself.

2.1 Apprehēnsī sunt adolēscentēs catēchūmenī: Revocātus et Fēlīcitās, cōnserva eius, Sāturnīnus et Secundulus. Inter hōs et Vibia Perpetua, honestē nāta, līberāliter īnstitūta, mātrōnāliter nūpta,

---

adolēscēns, -entis: young
āmēn: amen
annūntiō (1): to announce, proclaim
apprehendō, -ere, apprehendī, apprehēnsum: to seize; arrest
catēchūmenus, -ī m.: a catechumen (a Christian who has not yet been baptized)
clāritās, -tātis f.: brightness; glory
commūniō, -ōnis f.: association, communion
cōnserva, -ae f.: fellow slave
contrectō (1): to touch, handle (spelled *contractō* in Classical Latin)
fīliolus, -ī m.: little son
honestē: honorably, respectably
honor, -ōris m.: honor, glory

īnstituō, -ere, -uī, -ūtum: to set up; educate
intersum, -esse, -fuī: to take part in, be present
līberāliter: like a free person; nobly; liberally
martyr, -tyris m.: witness; martyr
mātrōnāliter: like a matron
nāscor, nāscī, nātus sum: to be born
nūbō, -ere, nūpsī, nūptum: to veil; marry
rememor (1): to remember (+ *gen.*)
Revocātus, -ī m.: Revocatus (on Revocatus and the other figures arrested with Perpetua, see Introduction IV.C)
Sāturnīnus, -ī m.: Saturninus
Secundulus, -ī m.: Secundulus
Vibia, -ae f.: Vibia (the name for any female member of Vibian family)

(id) quod audīvimus: *that which we have heard;* the *quod* is a relative pronoun here. In this sentence the Redactor quotes from the biblical letter 1 John but changes the words in a few places; only the directly quoted material is italicized
frātrēs et fīliolī: *brothers and little sons;* the Redactor added this vocative to the original quotation
quī ... et quī: the Redactor added these relative clauses to the original quotation; the first group is those who were present (*interfuistis*) for the martyrdom and the second is those who are learning of it second-hand (*per audītum,* lit. "through it having been heard")
sānctīs martyribus: *the holy martyrs;* the Redactor changed the original "in communion with us" to "in communion with the holy martyrs"
per illōs: *through them;* that is, through the martyrs
in saecula saeculōrum: *into the ages of ages;* that is, "forever and ever"

2. habēns patrem et mātrem et frātrēs duōs, alterum aequē catēchūmenum, et filium īnfantem ad ūbera. 3. Erat autem ipsa circiter annōrum vīgintī duo. Haec ōrdinem tōtum martyriī suī iam hinc ipsa nārrāvit sīcut cōnscrīptum manū suā et suō sēnsū relīquit.

Perpetua begins her narrative with an argument she had with her father while under house arrest. She is then taken to prison.

3.1 Cum adhūc (inquit) cum prōsecūtōribus essem et mē pater verbīs ēvertere cupīret et dēicere prō suā affectiōne persevērāret, "Pater," inquam, "vidēs verbī grātiā vās hoc iacēns, urceolum sīve aliud?"

---

aequē: equally; likewise
affectiō, -tiōnis f.: feeling, attitude
alter, -tera, -terum: one (or the other) of two
circiter: around, about
cupiō, -ere, -īvī, -ītum: to desire
ēvertō, -ere, -ī, -sum: to overturn
hinc: from here
iaceō, -ēre, -cuī: to lie down
martyrium, -iī n.: testimony; martyrdom
nārrō (1): to narrate, relate
ōrdō, -dinis m.: order, line, series (of events)

persevērō (1): to continue, persist
prōsecūtor, -ōris m.: prosecutor; escort
sēnsus, -ūs m.: feeling, sense; perception
sīcut: just as
sīve, seu: whether, or (if)
tōtus, -a, -um: whole, entire
ūber, -beris n.: breast
urceolus, -ī m.: litter pitcher, little pot
vās, vāsis n.: vessel
vīgintī duo, -ae, -o: twenty-two

---

annōrum vīgintī duo: *she was twenty-two (of) years;* gen. of description
Haec ... ipsa: *This woman ... herself;* these words refer to Perpetua, who is the subject of *nārrāvit* and *relīquit*
sīcut cōnscrīptum manū suā et suō sēnsū relīquit: *just as she left it written in her own hand and from her own perspective*
inquit: *she said;* the Redactor added *inquit* to signal to readers that this is the start of Perpetua's narrative
Cum ... essem: *While I was ...;* Perpetua's narrative begins while she is under house arrest
cupīret: this verb is fourth conjugation here, but is more regularly an *-iō* third conjugation verb
dēicere: *to throw down;* this verb (and *ēvertere*) would typically be used in reference to wrestling or physical combat, but here Perpetua uses them metaphorically, as she does throughout her narrative
prō suā affectiōne: *because of his affection;* lit. "in accordance with his affection"
persevērāret: this verb is subjunctive because it is in a circumstantial *cum*-clause (coordinated with *essem*)
verbī grātiā: *for the sake of example*

Et dīxit, "Videō."

2. Et ego dīxī eī, "Numquid aliō nōmine vocārī potest quam quod est?"
Et ait, "Nōn."

"Sīc et ego aliud mē dīcere nōn possum nisi quod sum, Chrīstiāna."

3. Tunc pater mōtus hōc verbō mittit sē in mē ut oculōs mihi ērueret,
sed vexāvit tantum et profectus est, victus cum argūmentīs Diabolī. 4.
Tunc paucīs diēbus quod caruissem patrem, Dominō grātiās ēgī et
refrīgerāvī absentiā illīus. 5. In ipsō spatiō paucōrum diērum baptīzātī
sumus, et mihi Spīritus dictāvit nōn aliud petendum ab aquā nisi
sufferentiam carnis. Post paucōs diēs recipimur in carcerem;

---

absentia, -ae f.: absence
āiō: to say, affirm (*ait* 3rd/sg./pres.)
argūmentum, -ī n.: proof, argument
baptīzō (1): to immerse; baptize
careō, -ēre, caruī: to be without, lack
Chrīstiānus, -a, -um: Christian
Diabolus, -ī m.: Satan (Grk. Slanderer)
dictō (1): to say
ēruō, -ere, ēruī, ērutum: to tear out
moveō, -ēre, mōvī, mōtum: to move, rouse

nōmen, nōminis n.: name
numquid: surely … not?
oculus, -ī m.: eye
proficīscor, -ī, profectus sum: to set out, leave
recipiō, -ere, recēpī, receptum: to take back; to take (into a place)
sufferentia, -ae f.: suffering, endurance
vexō (1): to agitate, shake, move violently
vincō, -ere, vīcī, victum: to conquer, defeat

Videō: *I see it;* repeating a verb from a question is a way of saying "yes"
quam quod est: *than what it is;* the *quam* is comparative; *quod* is the relative pronoun
ego aliud … sum: *I am not able to call myself another thing except what I am;* the *mē* is a direct
   object of the complementary infinitive *dīcere; quod* is a relative pronoun
ut … ērueret: *like he would tear my eyes out;* purpose clause; lit. "to tear out my eyes"
tantum: *only;* take closely with *vexāvit*
victus … Diabolī: *defeated along with the arguments of the Devil;* perfect passive participle with abl.
   of accompaniment
paucīs diēbus: *for a few days;* abl. of extent of time (see Introduction VI.A)
quod … patrem: the *quod* could mean "because" but it is more likely "when"; it typically takes the
   indicative but can take the subjunctive with no real difference in meaning
caruissem: *I was lacking;* in later Latin a pluperfect subjunctive often has an imperfect meaning; this
   verb takes an abl. object in Classical Latin but an acc. in later Latin
grātiās ēgī: *I gave thanks;* common idiom, *agere + grātiās*, "to give thanks"
refrīgerāvī: *I was refreshed;* the verb *refrīgerāre* can have an active sense ("to refresh") or a passive
   sense ("to be refreshed")
dictāvit: *dictāre* was a frequentative verb that meant "to say repeatedly," but at this point in time it
   has lost frequentative meaning
nōn aliud petendum (esse): *that nothing else ought to be sought;* literally "that another thing is not
   to be sought"

et expāvī, quia numquam experta eram tālēs tenebrās. 6. Ō diem asperum: aestus validus turbārum beneficiō; concussūrae mīlitum.

Novissimē mācerābar sollicitūdine īnfantis ibi. 7. Tunc Tertius et Pompōnius, benedictī diāconī quī nōbīs ministrābant, cōnstituērunt praemiō ut paucīs hōrīs ēmissī in meliōrem locum carceris refrīgerārēmus. 8. Tunc exeuntēs dē carcere ūniversī sibi vacābant. Ego īnfantem lactābam iam inediā dēfectum; sollicita prō eō adloquēbar mātrem et cōnfortābam frātrem, commendābam filium. Tābēscēbam ideō quod illōs tābēscere vīderam meī beneficiō. 9. Tālēs sollicitūdinēs multīs diēbus passa sum; et ūsurpāvī ut mēcum īnfāns in carcere manēret;

---

adloquor, -quī, -locūtus sum: to address, speak to

aestus, -ūs m.: heat, glow, fire

asper, aspera, asperum: harsh, rough

benedictus, -a, -um: blessed

commendō (1): to entrust, deposit with

concussūra, -ae f.: shaking; extortion

cōnfortō (1): to strengthen

cōnstituō, -ere, -uī, -ūtum: to arrange

dēficiō, -ere, -fēcī, -fectum: to fail, exhaust

diāconus, -ī m.: deacon

ēmittō, -ere, -mīsī, -missum: to send forth

expavēscō, -ere, expāvī: to panic, be terrified

experior, -īrī, -rtus sum: to experience

hōra, -ae f.: hour

inedia, -ae f.: lack of food, starvation

lactō (1): to nurse

mācerō (1): to weaken, make soft

maneō, -ēre, mānsī: to remain, await

melior, melius: better

ministrō (1): to minister, attend to, serve

numquam: never

Pompōnius, -ī m.: Pomponius (a deacon)

praemium, -iī n.: reward, prize; bribe

sollicitūdō, -inis f.: anxiety, worry

sollicitus, -a, -um: anxious, worried

tābēscō, -ere, tābuī: to melt, waste away, languish

tenebrae, -ārum f.: darkness

Tertius, -ī m.: Tertius (a deacon)

turba, -ae f.: crowd

ūsurpō (1): to use; to obtain (here: to obtain the right to do something)

vacō (1): to be empty, be vacant; have free time

validus, -a, -um: strong

Ō diem asperum: *What a rough day!;* acc. of exclamation

turbārum beneficiō: *because of the crowds; beneficiō* + genitive ("because of") is an idiom

concussūrae: *the shakedowns;* plural nom.

Novissimē: *finally;* superlative adverb; *novus* can mean "new," but also "recent" or "final"

cōnstituērunt praemiō: *they arranged, for a price;* basically a bribe

paucīs hōrīs: *for a few hours;* abl. of extent of time (see Introduction VI.A)

commendābam filium (illīs): *I entrusted my son to them;* to Perpetua's mother and brother

meī beneficiō: *because of me;* again the idiom *beneficiō* + genitive ("because of")

multīs diēbus: *for many days;* abl. of extent of time (see Introduction VI.A)

et statim convaluī et relevāta sum ā labōre et sollicitūdine īnfantis, et factus est mihi carcer subitō praetōrium, ut ibi māllem esse quam alicubi.

Perpetua narrates a vision: a bronze ladder to heaven, full of danger.

4.1 Tunc dīxit mihi frāter meus: "Domina soror, iam in magnā dignātiōne es, tantā ut postulēs vīsiōnem et ostendātur tibi an passiō sit an commeātus."

2. Et ego, quae mē sciēbam fābulārī cum Dominō, cuius beneficiō tanta experta eram, fidenter reprōmīsī eī dīcēns: "Crastinā diē tibi renūntiābō." Et postulāvī, et ostēnsum est mihi hoc:

3. Videō scālam aeream mīrae magnitūdinis pertingentem ūsque ad caelum et angustam, per quam nōnnisi singulī ascendere possent,

---

aereus, -a, -um: of bronze, brazen
alicubi: anywhere
angustus, -a, -um: narrow
commeātus, -ūs m.: a free pass; the ability to leave
convalēscō, -ere, convaluī: to recover
crastinus, -a, -um: (of) tomorrow
dignātiō, -tiōnis f.: esteem; grace
domina, -ae f.: master; lady (a term of respect for superiors)
experior, -īrī, -rtus sum: to experience
fābulor, -ārī, -ātum sum: to speak, converse
fidenter: confidently, boldly

labor, -ōris m.: labor, hardship
magnitūdō, -inis f.: magnitude, size
mīrus, -a, -um: wonderful, marvelous
nōnnisi: not unless, only
pertingō, -ere: to reach, extend, stretch out
praetōrium, -ī n.: officer's residence; palace
relevō (1): to lift up, raise; ease, relieve
renūntiō (1): to bring back word, report
reprōmittō, -ere, -mīsī, -missum: to promise in return
singulī, -ae, -a: one by one, individuals
sollicitūdō, -inis f.: anxiety, worry
subitō: suddenly

---

factus est ... carcer ... praetōrium: *the prison became a palace;* the subject is *carcer* and *praetōrium* the predicate subject
frāter meus: probably "brother" in the sense of fellow-Christian rather than biological sibling
in magnā ... tantā ut: *you are in great grace, so great that;* the *tantā* is ablative in agreement with *dignātiōne*, the *ut* introduces a result clause
an passiō sit an commeātus: *whether it will be suffering or a free pass;* that is, whether they will be killed or released
quae mē sciēbam fābulārī: *since I knew that I spoke;* lit. "I, who knew that I spoke"
Crastinā diē: *tomorrow;* lit. "on tomorrow's day"; abl. of time when
Videō: Perpetua switches to present tense when describing her visions (cf. 7.4, 8.1, and 10.1)
pertingentem ... angustam: both agree with *scālam aeream*
per quam nōnnisi singulī ascendere possent: *which could only be climbed single file;* lit. "through which only individuals could climb"

41

et in lateribus scālae omne genus ferrāmentōrum īnfixum. Erant ibi gladiī, lanceae, hāmī, macherae, ut sī quis neglegenter aut nōn sūrsum adtendēns ascenderet, laniārētur et carnēs eius inhaerērent ferrāmentīs. 4. Et erat sub ipsā scālā dracō cubāns mīrae magnitūdinis, quī ascendentibus īnsidiās praestābat et exterrēbat nē ascenderent.

5. Ascendit autem Satūrus prior, quī posteā sē propter nōs ultrō trādiderat (quia ipse nōs aedificāverat), et tunc cum adductī sumus, praesēns nōn fuerat. 6. Et pervēnit in caput scālae et convertit sē et dīxit mihi: "Perpetua, sustineō tē; sed vidē nē tē mordeat dracō ille."

Et dīxī ego: "Nōn mē nocēbit, in nōmine Iēsū Chrīstī."

---

addūcō, -ere, -dūxī, -ductum: to lead to, bring
adtendō, -ere, -tendī, -tentum: to stretch, turn to, look
aedificō (1): to build; instruct
convertō, -ere, -ī, -versum: to turn
cubō (1): to lie down, recline, sleep
dracō, -ōnis m.: serpent
exterreō, -ēre, -uī, -itum: to terrify
ferrāmentum, -ī n.: iron tool, ironworks
genus, -eris n.: kind, sort
hāmus, -ī m.: hook
īnfīgō, -ere, -xī, -xum: to stick on, attach
inhaereō, -ēre, -haesī, -haesum: to stick on, cling
īnsidiae, -ārum f.: ambush; threat
lancea, -ae f.: light spear, lance

laniō (1): to tear to pieces, mangle, lacerate
latus, -eris n.: side
mach(a)era, -ae f.: sword
magnitūdō, -tūdinis f.: magnitude, size
mīrus, -a, -um: wonderful, marvelous
mordeō, -ēre, momordī, morsum: to bite
neglegenter: negligently, carelessly
noceō, -ēre, -uī, -itum: to harm, inflict injury
posteā: afterwards
praesēns, -entis: present
praestō, -āre, -stitī, -stitum: to show oneself as (+ acc.)
sūrsum: upwards
sustineō, -ēre, -uī, sustentus: to support; await
trādō, -dere, -didī, -ditum: to give up, hand over
ultrō: beyond; voluntarily, of one's will

---

sī quis: *if anybody;* the *quis* is shortened from *aliquis,* as usual following *sī, nisi, num,* or *nē*
neglegenter … adtendēns: *(either) carelessly or not looking upwards;* these two items are coordinated: they are the two possibilities under which one would get mangled while ascending
sē … trādiderat: *of his own will handed himself over because of us;* that is, he turned himself in because he had taught the group of catechumens
adductī sumus: *we were arrested;* lit. "we were brought (to the authorities)"
sustineō: this verb takes on a double meaning here: Satyrus is both waiting for Perpetua to ascend the ladder and expressing his support for her
vidē nē … dracō ille: *do not let that serpent bite you;* lit. "see that the serpent doesn't bite you"; *vidē nē* + subjunctive forms a negative imperative
Nōn mē nocēbit: *it will not harm me;* the verb *nocēre* here takes the accusative rather than the dative expected in Classical Latin (see Introduction VI.D)
Iēsū: *of Jesus;* this form is the genitive of *Iēsus* (= Grk. Ἰησοῦ)

7. Et dēsub ipsā scālā, quasi timēns mē, lentē ēiēcit caput. Et quasi prīmum gradum calcārem, calcāvī illī caput et ascendī. 8. Et vīdī spatium immēnsum hortī et in mediō sedentem hominem cānum in habitū pāstōris, grandem, ovēs mulgentem. Et circumstantēs candidātī, mīlia multa. 9. Et levāvit caput et aspexit mē et dīxit mihi: "Bene vēnistī, *tegnon*." Et clāmāvit mē et dē cāseō quod mulgēbat dedit mihi quasi buccellam; et ego accēpī iūnctīs manibus et mandūcāvī; et ūniversī circumstantēs dīxērunt "Āmēn."

10. Et ad sonum vōcis experrēcta sum, commandūcāns adhūc dulce nesciōquid.

---

buccella, -ae f.: small mouthful, morsel
candidātus, -a, -um: white-robed
cāseum, -ī n.: cheese (masc. *caseus* in Classical Latin)
circumstō, -āre, -stetī: to stand around
clāmō (1): to shout, call out to
commandūcō (1): to chew
dēsub: below, beneath (+ *abl.*)
dulcis, -e: sweet
ēiciō, -ere, -iēcī, -iectum: to cast out, put out
expergīscor, expergīscī, experrēctus sum: to wake
gradus, -ūs m.: step
grandis, -e: large; great; old
habitus, -ūs m.: dress, attire
hortus, -ī m.: garden
iungō, -ere, iūnxī, iūnctum: to join, attach

lentē: slowly
levō (1): to lift up, raise up
mandūcō (1): to chew, masticate, eat, devour
medium, -ī n.: the middle
mīlle *pl.* mīlia, -ium n.: thousand
mulgeō, -ēre, -lsī, -lsum: to milk
nescioquis, nescioquid: something (I do not know what)
ovis, -is f.: sheep
pāstor, pāstōris m.: shepherd
prīmus, -a, -um: first
sedeō, -ēre, sēdī, sessum: to sit
sonus, -ī m.: sound
tegnon: child (vocative of Grk. τέκνον)
timeō, -ēre, timuī: to fear
vōx, vōcis f.: voice; utterance, word

---

timēns: agrees with an implied *draco*
illī caput: *his head;* a dat. is commonly used with body parts rather than a possessive adj. or gen.
in habitū pāstōris: *in the attire of a shepherd;* Jesus is often depicted as a shepherd in early Christian art and literature
Et circumstantēs (erant) candidātī, mīlia multa: *And standing around (us) were people dressed in white, many thousands (of them);* the *candidātī* is the subject and *circumstantēs* the predicate; *mīlia multa* is in apposition to *candidātī* but is neuter since "thousand" only has neuter forms in the plural
Bene vēnistī: *welcome*
dē cāseō ... buccellam: suggestive of the Christian ritual of *Thanksgiving* (see Introduction V.A)
quasi buccellam: *about a mouthful;* the word *quasi* can have a sense "nearly" or "almost"
ad sonum: *at the sound*
experrēcta sum: *I awoke;* the standard way in this narrative for a vision to end (cf. 7.9, 8.4, 10.13, and 13.8)

Et retulī statim frātrī meō; et intellēximus passiōnem esse futūram, et coepimus nūllam iam spem in saeculō habēre.

Perpetua's father pleads with her, but she is resolute.

5.1 Post paucōs diēs rūmor cucurrit ut audīrēmur. Supervēnit autem et dē cīvitāte pater meus, cōnsūmptus taediō, et ascendit ad mē, ut mē dēiceret, dīcēns: 2 "Miserēre, fīlia, cānīs meīs; miserēre patrī, sī dignus sum ā tē pater vocārī. Sī hīs tē manibus ad hunc flōrem aetātis prōvēxī, sī tē praeposuī omnibus frātribus tuīs, nē mē dederīs in dēdecus hominum. 3. Aspice frātrēs tuōs, aspice mātrem tuam et māterteram, aspice fīlium tuum quī post tē vīvere nōn poterit.

---

aetās, aetātis f.: age, life
cīvitās, cīvitātis f.: city
cōnsūmō, -ere, cōnsūmpsī, cōnsūmptum: to consume
currō, -ere, cucurrī, cursum: to run, rush, fly
dēdecus, -oris n.: disgrace, dishonor, shame
dignus, -a, -um: worthy
flōs, flōris m.: flower, blossom
mātertera, -ae f.: aunt (mother's sister)
misereor, -ērī, -itus sum: to pity, have mercy on (+ *dat.*)

nūllus, -a, -um: none, no, no one
praepōnō, -ere, praeposuī, praepositum: to place in front (+ *dat.*)
prōvehō, -ere, prōvēxī, prōvectum: to carry forward, move, advance
referō, -ferre, -tulī, -lātum: to report
rūmor, -ōris m.: rumor
superveniō, -īre, -vēnī, -ventum: to arrive (unexpectedly)
taedium, -ī n.: weariness
vīvō, -ere, vīxī, vīctum: to live

---

in saeculō: *in this world;* the word *saeculum* here (lit. "age") meaning the present world, as often in early Christian texts
ut audīrēmur: *that we would have a hearing;* lit. "that we would be heard"; this clause is a noun clause in apposition to *rūmor*
ut mē dēiceret: *to throw me down;* Perpetua again uses the language of wrestling
Miserēre ... miserēre: *have mercy;* second person singular imperative of *misereor*, a deponent verb; here this verb takes the dative, though in Classical Latin it takes the genitive (see Introduction VI.D)
Sī hīs ... prōvēxī: *If I raised you up with these hands to this blossom of life;* the phrase *flōs aetātis* is an idiom for "the prime of life"
nē mē dederīs in dēdecus: *do not deliver me into dishonor;* jussive subjunctives often use the perfect tense in second person
aspice fīlium ... poterit: *Look at your son, who will not be able to live after you (die);* the father could be saying that her son will not flourish without her, but he could also be threatening to use his right to kill or abandon the child unless she yields

4. "Dēpōne animōs; nē ūniversōs nōs exterminēs. Nēmō enim nostrum līberē loquētur, sī tū aliquid fueris passa."

5. Haec dīcēbat pater prō suā pietāte, bāsiāns mihi manūs et sē ad pedēs meōs iactāns; et lacrymīs mē iam nōn filiam nōminābat, sed dominam. 6. Et ego dolēbam cāsum patris meī quod sōlus dē passiōne meā gāvīsūrus nōn esset dē tōtō genere meō. Et cōnfortāvī eum dīcēns, "Hoc fiet in illā catastā quod Deus voluerit. Scītō enim nōs nōn in nostrā esse potestāte cōnstitūtōs, sed in Deī." Et recessit ā mē contrīstātus.

Perpetua's trial: she refuses to sacrifice to the emperors.

6.1 Aliō diē cum prandērēmus, subitō raptī sumus ut audīrēmur.

---

animus, -ī m.: mind, spirit; courage, pride (*pl.*)
bāsiō (1): to kiss
cāsus, -ūs m.: misfortune; fate
catasta, -ae f.: platform
cōnfortō (1): to strengthen; comfort
cōnstituō, -ere, -uī, -ūtum: to arrange; decide
contrīstō (1): to sadden, cast gloom over
dēpōnō, -ere, -posuī, -positum: to set aside
domina, -ae f.: master; lady (term of respect for a superior)
exterminō (1): to put an end; destroy
genus, generis n.: family, kind, sort
iactō (1): to throw

lacryma, -ae f.: tear
līberē: freely
loquor, loquī, locūtus sum: to speak, say
nēmō, nēminis: no one
nōminō (1): to name, to call
pietās, pietātis f.: devotion
potestās, -tātis f.: power
prandeō, -ēre, -dī: to eat lunch, eat
rapiō, -ere, rapuī, raptum: to seize
recēdō, -ere, -cessī, -cessum: to depart
sōlus, -a, -um: alone
subitō: suddenly
tōtus, -a, -um: whole, entire

---

nē ... exterminēs: *do not destroy us all;* jussive subjunctive
Nēmō ... nostrum: *no one of us;* partitive genitive
sī tū aliquid fueris passa: *if you suffer anything;* fueris passa = eris passa (see Introduction VI.F); the condition is future more vivid
prō suā pietāte: *because of his devotion;* lit. "in accordance with his devotion"
quod sōlus ... dē tōtō genere meō: *because he alone ... out of all my family*
gāvīsūrus nōn esset: *would not rejoice;* Perpetua uses a future active participle with *sum* since there is no future tense in the subjunctive
Hoc fiet ... quod Deus voluerit: *What will happen on that platform is what God has willed;* lit. "This thing will happen ... which God has willed"
Scītō: *Know;* future imperative of *scīre*
in deī (potestāte): *but in (the power) of God*
ut audīrēmur: *for our (judicial) hearing;* lit. "in order that we might be heard"

Et pervēnimus ad forum. Rūmor statim per vīcīnās forī partēs cucurrit et factus est populus immēnsus. 2. Ascendimus in catastam. Interrogātī, cēterī cōnfessī sunt. Ventum est et ad mē. Et appāruit pater īlicō cum fīliō meō et extrāxit mē dē gradū, supplicāns: "Miserēre īnfantī."

3. Et Hilariānus prōcūrātor, quī tunc locō prōcōnsulis Minūcī Timīniānī dēfūnctī iūs gladiī accēperat, "Parce," inquit, "cānīs patris tuī, parce īnfantiae puerī. Fac sacrum prō salūte imperātōrum."

4. Et ego respondī, "Nōn faciō."

Hilariānus "Chrīstiāna es?" inquit.

Et ego respondī, "Chrīstiāna sum."

---

appāreō, -ēre, appāruī, -itum: to appear
catasta, -ae f.: platform
Chrīstiānus, -a, -um: Christian
cōnfiteor, cōnfitērī, cōnfessus sum: to confess
currō, -ere, cucurrī, cursus: to run, rush, fly
dēfungor, -ī, -fūnctus sum: to die, finish
extrahō, -ere, -trāxī, -tractum: to drag off
forum, -ī n.: forum, marketplace
gradus, -ūs m.: step
īlicō: there, right there
imperātor, -ōris m.: commander; emperor
īnfantia, -ae f.: infancy
interrogō (1): to ask, question, interrogate
iūs, iūris n.: law, right

Minūcius, -ī m.: Minucius
misereor, -ērī, -itus sum: to pity (+ *dat.*)
parcō, -ere, pepercī: to spare (+ *dat.*)
pars, partis f.: part
prōcōnsul, -lis m.: proconsul, the official in charge of the province
prōcūrātor, -ōris m.: procurator, a senior administrator
rūmor, -ōris m.: rumor
sacrum, -ī n.: a sacrifice
salūs, -ūtis f.: safety; health
supplicō (1): to fall to one's knees; beg
Timīniānus, -ī m.: Timinianus
vīcīnus, -a, -um: neighboring

---

factus est populus immēnsus: *a huge crowd gathered;* the *factus est* is literally "was made" (from *fīō, fierī, factus sum*); the word *populus* means "crowd" here and elsewhere in the *Passiō*
Ventum est: *it came;* impersonal passive
Miserēre īnfantī: *Pity your child;* second person singular imperative of *misereor,* a deponent verb; here this verb takes the dative, though in Classical Latin it takes the genitive
Hilariānus: Publius Aelius Hilarianus, an equestrian (see Introduction IV.D)
locō prōcōnsulis Minūcī Timīniānī dēfūnctī: *in place of the deceased proconsul, Minucius Timinianus;* on the name see Introduction IV.D
iūs gladiī: *right of the sword;* the right to carry out capital punishment
Fac sacrum prō salūte imperātōrum: *Perform a sacrifice for the health of the emperors;* in 203 CE the emperors were Septimius Severus (r. 193-211) and his son Caracalla (r. 198-217)

5. Et cum stāret pater ad mē dēiciendam, iussus est ab Hilariānō dēicī, et virgā percussus est. Et doluit mihi cāsus patris meī quasi ego fuissem percussa; sīc doluī prō senectā eius miserā. 6. Tunc nōs ūniversōs prōnūntiat, et damnat ad bēstiās; et hilarēs dēscendimus ad carcerem. 7. Tunc quia cōnsuēverat ā mē īnfāns mammās accipere et mēcum in carcere manēre, statim mittō ad patrem Pompōnium diāconum, postulāns īnfantem. Sed pater dare nōluit. 8. Et quōmodo Deus voluit, neque ille amplius mammās dēsīderāvit, neque mihi fervōrem fēcērunt nē sollicitūdine īnfantis et dolōre mammārum mācerārer.

---

amplius: more, longer (*comp. adv.*)
cāsus, -ūs m.: misfortune; fate
cōnsuēscō, -ere, -suēvī, -suētum: to be accustomed
damnō (1): to condemn
dēiciō, -ere, -iēcī, -iectum: to throw down; dissuade
dēscendō, -ere, -ndī, -nsum: to descend
dēsīderō (1): to long for; require
diāconus, -ī m.: assistant; deacon
doleō, -ēre, -uī, -itum: to feel pain; to cause pain
fervor, -ōris m.: boiling heat, raging heat
hilaris, -e: cheerful, joyous
iubeō, -ēre, iussī, iussum: to order, bid

mācerō (1): to weaken; torment
mamma, -ae f.: breast
maneō, -ēre, mānsī, mānsum: to remain, await
miser, misera, miserum: wretched, pitiable
percutiō, -ere, -cussī, -cussum: to strike, beat
Pompōnius, -ī m.: Pomponius
prōnūntiō (1): to pronounce; sentence
senecta, -ae f.: old age
sollicitūdō, -inis f.: anxiety
statim: immediately
stō, stāre, stetī, statum: to stand; stand firm
virga, -ae f.: rod

Et cum stāret pater ad mē dēiciendam: *And when my father stood (firm in his determination) to change my mind;* the verb *stāre* here has a metaphorical sense of "stand firm," *dēicere* a metaphorical sense of "to throw someone (off their position)"; the gerundive phrase *mē dēiciendam* ("me to be thrown down") is an idiomatic equivalent to a gerund with a direct object: *dēiciendum mē* ("throwing me down")

doluit mihi cāsus patris: *my father's misfortune pained me;* the verb *dolēre* can take a dative as its direct object

quasi ego fuissem percussa: *as if I myself had been beaten;* fuissem percussa = essem percussa (see Introduction VI.F)

neque mihi (mammae) fervōrem fēcērunt: *and my breasts were not feverish;* if nursing is stopped abruptly, breasts can become painful and feverish

sollicitūdine īnfantis: *anxiety for (my) child;* objective genitive

Perpetua relates a second vision: her brother suffering in the afterlife.

7.1 Post diēs paucōs, dum ūniversī ōrāmus, subitō mediā ōrātiōne profecta est mihi vōx, et nōmināvī Dīnocratēn. Et obstipuī quod numquam mihi in mentem vēnisset nisi tunc, et doluī commemorāta cāsūs eius. 2. Et cognōvī mē statim dignam esse et prō eō petere dēbēre. Et coepī dē ipsō ōrātiōnem facere multum et ingemiscere ad Dominum. 3. Continuō ipsā nocte ostēnsum est mihi hoc:

4. Videō Dīnocratēn exeuntem dē locō tenebrōsō ubi et complūrēs erant, aestuantem valdē et sitientem, sordidō vultū et colōre pallidō; et vulnus in faciē eius, quod cum morerētur habuit.

---

aestuō (1): to be burning hot
cāsus, -ūs m.: misfortune; fate
color, -ōris m.: color, complexion
commemorō (1): to recall (+ *gen.*)
complūrēs, -plūra: very many
continuō: immediately (*adv.*)
dēbeō, -ēre, -uī, dēbitum: to owe; ought
dignus, -a, -um: worthy
dum: while, as long as, until
ingemiscō, -ere, -uī: to groan, sigh, moan
mēns, mentis f.: mind
nōminō (1): to name, call by name, to call
nox, noctis, f.: night
numquam: never

obstipescō, -ere, obstipuī: to be astounded
ōrō (1): to plead; pray
pallidus, -a, -um: pale, pallid, bloodless
petō, -ere, petīvī, petītum: to ask; pray
proficīscor, -ī, profectus sum: to go out
sitiō, -īre, -īvī: to be thirsty, thirst
sordidus, -a, -um: dirty
subitō: suddenly
tenebrōsus, -a, -um: dark, gloomy
valdē: very, exceedingly
vōx, vōcis f.: voice; utterance, word
vulnus, -eris n.: wound
vultus, -ūs m.: face

---

mediā ōrātiōne: *in the midst of prayer;* abl. of time when
Dīnocratēn: Dinocrates is Perpetua's deceased brother; the form here is a Greek accusative
quod ... vēnisset: *because it had never come;* there is no clear reason for the subjunctive here (see Introduction VI.G)
commemorāta cāsūs eius: *remembering his fate;* the verb *commemorāre* sometimes uses passive forms with a middle sense ("to recall to one's own mind")
prō eō petere: *to pray for him;* the verb *petere* is most literally "seek" but can mean "pray" in early Christian texts
ōrātiōnem facere multum: *to pray repeatedly;* the *multum* here is an adverb ("greatly," "repeatedly")
ostēnsum ... hoc: *this was shown to me;* Perpetua uses this phrase to mark the beginning of new visions (cf. 4.2, 8.1)
Videō: Perpetua uses the present tense where the perfect would be expected so as to take readers through her vision as she experienced it (cf. 4.3, 8.1, 10.1)
sordidō vultū et colōre pallidō: *with a dirty face and pale complexion;* abl. of description
cum morerētur: *when he was dying;* imperfect subjunctive of *morior, morī, mortuus sum*

5. Hic Dīnocratēs fuerat frāter meus carnālis, annōrum septem, quī per īnfirmitātem faciē cancerātā male obiit ita ut mors eius odiō fuerit omnibus hominibus. 6. Prō hōc ergō ōrātiōnem fēceram; et inter mē et illum grande erat diastēma ita ut uterque ad invicem accēdere nōn possēmus. 7. Erat deinde in ipsō locō ubi Dīnocratēs erat piscīna plēna aquā, altiōrem marginem habēns quam erat statūra puerī; et extendēbat sē Dīnocratēs quasi bibitūrus. 8. Ego dolēbam quod et piscīna illa aquam habēbat et tamen propter altitūdinem marginis bibitūrus nōn esset.

---

altior, -ius: higher, taller (*altus*)
altitūdō, -dinis f.: height, depth
bibō, -ere, bibī: to drink (fut. act. participle bibitūrus, -a, -um)
cancerāscō, -ere, cancerāvī, cancerātus: to become cancerous, be afflicted with cancer
carnālis, -e: of the flesh
deinde: then; moreover
diastēma, -matis n.: interval, space (between)
ergō: therefore
extendō, -ere, extendī, extentum (extēnsum): to stretch, spread out

grandis, -e: large, great
īnfirmitās, -tātis f.: weakness; sickness
male: badly; tragically
mors, mortis f.: death
obeō, -īre, -iī (-īvī), -itum: to die, pass away
odium, -iī n.: hatred; loathing
piscīna, -ae f.: pool
plēnus, -a, -um: full, filled with (+ *abl.*)
septem: seven
statūra, -ae f.: stature, size, height
uterque, utraque, utrumque: each (of two), both

---

frāter meus carnālis: *biological brother;* Perpetua specifies *carnālis* to avoid ambiguity between a biological brother and fellow Christians
annōrum septem: *seven years old;* lit. "(a boy) of seven years"; gen. of description dependent on *Dīnocratēs*
faciē cancerātā: *from a cancer in the face;* lit. "from a cancered face"; abl. of means
ita ut: *in such a way that;* begins a result clause governed by *obiit*
odiō ... omnibus hominibus: *a source of loathing for all;* the *odiō* is dat. of purpose, and *omnibus hominibus* is dat. of reference; together they form a double dative construction
Prō ... fēceram: *I prayed on his behalf;* lit. "I made a prayer on behalf of this (child)"
invicem: *each other;* used in place of a reflexive pronoun
altiōrem ... puerī: *having an edge higher than was the height of the boy;* the *habēns* modifies *piscīna* and has direct object *marginem*, which is compared to *statūra puerī* with *altiōrem quam* (comparative + *quam*)
quasi bibitūrus: *as if desiring to drink;* future active participle here expressing intention
dolēbam quod: *I was sad because;* the *quod* acts as a conjunction, not as a relative pronoun
bibitūrus ... esset: *he would not be able to drink;* the future participle with *sum* is a future periphrastic form, equivalent to the non-existent future subjunctive

49

9. Et experrēcta sum, et cognōvī frātrem meum labōrāre. Sed fidēbam mē prōfutūram labōrī eius. Et ōrābam prō eō omnibus diēbus quōūsque trānsīvimus in carcerem castrēnsem. Mūnere enim castrēnsī erāmus pugnātūrī; nātāle tunc Getae Caesaris. 10. Et fēcī prō illō ōrātiōnem diē et nocte gemēns et lacrimāns ut mihi dōnārētur.

Perpetua relates a third vision: her brother no longer suffering.

8.1 Diē quō in nervō mānsimus, ostēnsum est mihi hoc:

Caesar, -aris m.: Caesar
castrēnsis, -e: of a military camp (*castra*)
dōnō (1): to give, grant
expergiscor, expergiscī, experrēctus sum: to wake
fīdō, -ere, fīsus sum: to trust
gemō, -ere, -uī, -itum: to groan, sigh
Geta, -ae m.: Geta
labor, -ōris m.: hardship, suffering
labōrō (1): to labor, struggle, suffer
lacrimō (1): to weep, cry

maneō, -ēre, mānsī, mānsum: to remain, stay
mūnus, -eris n.: duty, gift; gladiatorial games
nātāle, -is n.: birthday (masc. in Classical Latin)
nervus, -ī m.: fetter, cord; stocks
nox, noctis f.: night
ōrō (1): to plead; pray (for)
prōsum, prōdesse, prōfuī: to be useful, beneficial (fut. act. participle prōfutūrus, -a, -um)
quōūsque: until, up until
trānseō, -īre, -iī (-īvī), -itum: to go over

Et experrēcta sum, et cognōvī: *And I woke, and I understood;* the standard way in this narrative for a vision to end (cf. 4.10, 8.4, 10.13, and 13.8)
mē prōfutūram (esse) labōrī eius: *that I would be useful for his hardship;* the verb *prōsum* takes a dative object (*labōrī*)
omnibus diēbus: *every day;* abl. of extent of time (see Introduction VI.A)
Mūnere ... castrēnsī: Perpetua has been sentenced to die fighting beasts at the military games
nātāle tunc (erat) Getae Caesaris: *at that time it was the birthday of Geta Caesar;* the games are part of the birthday celebrations for Geta Caesar, who later became co-emperor with his brother, Caracalla, and their father, Septimius Severus
ut ... dōnārētur: an indirect command governed by *gemēns et lacrimāns;* the implied subject of *dōnārētur* is the prayer for Dinocrates
Diē quō: *On a day in which;* abl. of time when
ostēnsum ... hoc: *this was shown to me;* Perpetua uses this phrase to mark the beginning of new visions (cf. 4.2, 7.3)

Videō locum illum quem retrō vīderam et Dīnocratēn mundō corpore, bene vestītum, refrīgerantem; et ubi erat vulnus videō cicātrīcem, 2. et piscīnam illam, quam retrō vīderam, summissō margine ūsque ad umbilīcum puerī; et aquam dē eā trahēbat sine cessātiōne; 3. et super margine fiala aurea plēna aquā; et accessit Dīnocratēs et dē eā bibere coepit; quae fiala nōn dēficiēbat. 4. Et satiātus accessit dē aquā lūdere mōre īnfantium gaudēns.

Et experrēcta sum. Tunc intellēxī trānslātum eum esse dē poenā.

---

aureus, -a, -um: golden
bibō, -ere, bibī: to drink
cessātiō, -tiōnis f.: cessation, letup
cicātrīx, -trīcis f.: scar
corpus, corporis n.: body
dēficiō, -ere, -fēcī, -fectum: to fail, exhaust; empty
fiala, -ae f.: cup
lūdō, -ere, lūsī, lūsum: to play
mōs, mōris m.: custom, manner
mundus, -a, -um: pure, clean, elegant
piscīna, -ae f.: pool

plēnus, -a, -um: full, filled with (+ *abl.*)
poena, -ae f.: punishment; suffering
retrō: back; previously, before (*adv.*)
satiō (1): to satisfy, sate
summittō, -ere, -mīsī, -missum: to lower
trahō, -ere, trāxī, tractum: to draw
trānsferō, -ferre, -tulī, -lātum: to carry across, transport; free
umbilīcus, -ī m.: navel; middle
vestiō, -īre, -iī (-īvī), -ītum: to clothe, dress
vulnus, -eris n.: wound

Videō: Perpetua uses the present tense where the perfect would be expected so as to take readers through her vision as she experienced it (cf. 4.3, 7.4, 10.1)

locum … et Dīnocratēn: both are direct objects of *Videō*; the ending of *Dīnocratēn* is a Greek accusative

mundō corpore: *with a clean body;* abl. of description

refrīgerantem: *getting refreshment;* lit. "being refreshed"; the verb *refrīgerāre* can have an active sense ("to refresh") or a passive sense ("to be refreshed")

summissō … puerī: *with the edge having been lowered all the way to the boy's middle;* abl. absolute

(erat) fiala aurea: *there was a golden cup*

quae fiala: *and this cup;* lit. "which cup"

accessit: *began;* the verb *accēdere* is most literally "to approach" but can mean "undertake" or "begin"

dē aquā: *with the water;* unlike in Classical Latin, the abl. of means takes the preposition *dē* (see Introduction VI.C)

mōre īnfantium: *in the manner of children*

Et experrēcta sum. Tunc intellēxī: *And I woke. Then I understood;* the standard way in this narrative for a vision to end (cf. 4.10, 7.9, 10.13, and 13.8)

trānslātum … poenā: *that he had been freed from suffering;* the word *trānslātum* suggests that Dinocrates was transferred from one place to another, but it is not certain what these places are: Purgatory (or Hell) to Heaven? One part of Hades to another?

Perpetua's father visits, agonized, but he cannot change her mind.

9.1 Deinde post diēs paucōs Pudēns mīles, optiō praepositus carceris, quī nōs magnificāre coepit intellegēns magnam virtūtem esse in nōbīs, multōs ad nōs admittēbat ut et nōs et illī invicem refrīgerārēmus.

2. Ut autem proximāvit diēs mūneris, intrat ad mē pater meus cōnsūmptus taediō, et coepit barbam suam ēvellere, et in terram mittere, et prōsternere sē in faciem, et improperāre annīs suīs, et dīcere tanta verba quae movērent ūniversam creātūram. 3. Ego dolēbam prō īnfēlīcī senectā eius.

---

admittō, -ere, -mīsī, -missum: to admit, allow
annus, -ī m.: year
barba, -ae f.: beard
cōnsūmō, -ere, cōnsūmpsī, cōnsūmptum: to use up, consume
creātūra, -ae f.: creation
deinde: then, next
doleō, -ēre, -uī, -itum: to feel pain, grieve
ēvellō, -ere, ēvellī, ēvulsum: to tear or pull out
improperō (1): reproach, blame, curse (+ *dat.*)
īnfēlīx, -īcis: unhappy, unfortunate
intrō (1): go into, enter; come
magnificō (1): to think highly of

moveō, -ēre, mōvī, mōtum: to move, rouse
mūnus, mūneris n.: spectacle, gladiatorial games
optiō, -ōnis m.: centurion's assistant
praepōnō, -ere, praeposuī, praepositum: to place in front; place in command of (+ *gen.*)
prōsternō, -ere, prōstrāvī, prōstrātum: to throw down
proximō (1): to draw or come near, approach
Pudēns, Pudentis m.: Pudens (the warden)
senecta, -ae f.: old age
taedium, -ī n.: weariness

Pudēns mīles: Perpetua remarks on the behavior of Pudens because he later converts to Christianity (cf. 16.4, 21.1, 21.4)
magnam virtūtem: *great power;* the word *virtūs* here means "power," as is often the case in early Christian texts
multōs (hominēs): *many people*
invicem: *each other;* acting as a direct object of *refrīgerārēmus* and used in place of a reflexive pronoun, as is often the case in the *Passiō*
Ut autem: *Moreover, when*
tanta verba quae movērent ... creātūram: *such words as might move all creation;* relative clause of characteristic

Perpetua recounts a fourth vision: her battle in the arena.

10.1 Prīdiē quam pugnārēmus, videō in horōmate hoc: vēnisse Pompōnium diāconum ad ōstium carceris et pulsāre vehementer. 2. Et exīvī ad eum et aperuī eī; quī erat vestītus discīnctā candidā, habēns multiplicēs galliculās. 3. Et dīxit mihi: "Perpetua, tē expectāmus: venī!" Et tenuit mihi manum et coepimus īre per aspera loca et flexuōsa.

4. Vix tandem pervēnimus anhēlantēs ad amphitheātrum et indūxit mē in mediā arēnā et dīxit mihi: "Nōlī pavēre. Hīc sum tēcum et conlabōrō tēcum." Et abiit.

---

abeō, -īre, -īvī, -itum: to go away, depart
amphitheātrum, -ī n.: amphitheater, arena
anhēlō (1): to pant
aperiō, -īre, aperuī, apertum: to open; reveal
arēna, -ae f.: sand; arena
asper, aspera, asperum: harsh, rough
candidus, -a, -um: bright white, white
conlabōrō (1): to labor with, struggle together
diāconus, -ī m.: deacon
discīngō, -ere, -xī, -nctum: to unbelt, loosen
exspectō (1): to wait for, await, look for
flexuōsus, -a, -um: winding, crooked
gallicula, -ae f.: Gallic shoe
hīc: here

horōma, -matis n.: a vision
indūcō, -ere, indūxī, inductum: to lead or bring in
multiplex, -plicis: manifold, many
ōstium, -iī n.: entrance, opening
paveō, -ēre, pāvī: to panic, be terrified, fear
Pompōnius, -ī m.: Pomponius (a deacon)
prīdiē: on the day before, the previous day
pulsō (1): to strike against, knock
tandem: finally, at last
teneō, tenēre, tenuī, tentum: to hold, keep
vehementer: vehemently, strongly, violently
vestiō, -īre, -īvī, -ītum: to clothe, dress
vix: with difficulty, with effort, scarcely

Prīdiē quam pugnārēmus: *On the day before we were going to fight;* the *quam* here is comparative and is often idiomatically paired with *prīdiē*, though it is best left out of translation

videō: Perpetua uses the present tense where the perfect would be expected so as to take readers through her vision as she experienced it (cf. 4.3, 7.4, 8.1)

vēnisse Pompōnium diāconum … et pulsāre: *that Pomponius the deacon had come … and was knocking;* Perpetua begins with an ind. statement and switches to simple indicative at 10.2

quī: *and he (Pomponius);* lit. "who"

discīnctā candidā (tunicā): *an unbelted white (tunic)*

multiplicēs galliculās: *strappy sandals;* it is not clear exactly how these sandals are "manifold" (*multiplicēs*), but it suggests some kind of elaborate footwear

venī: *come!;* imperative

mihi manum: *my hand;* the dative is commonly used to express possession with body parts

aspera loca et flexuōsa: *rough and winding places*

in mediā arēnā: *into the middle (of the) arena;* here in + abl. indicates motion towards (see Introduction VI.B)

Nōlī pavēre: *Do not fear;* standard form of the negative imperative

5. Et aspiciō populum ingentem attonitum; et quia sciēbam mē ad bēstiās damnātam esse, mīrābar quod nōn mitterentur mihi bēstiae. 6. Et exīvit quīdam contrā mē Aegyptius foedus speciē cum adiūtōribus suīs pugnātūrus mēcum. Veniunt et ad mē adolescentēs decōrī, adiūtōrēs et faūtōrēs meī. 7. Et expoliāta sum et facta sum masculus; et coepērunt mē faūtōrēs meī oleō dēfricāre, quōmodo solent in agōnem. Et illum contrā Aegyptium videō in afā volūtantem.

---

adiūtor, -ōris m.: helper
adolēscēns, -entis m./f.: a young person
afa, -ae f.: dust; sand
agōn, -ōnis m.: struggle; contest; fight
aspiciō, -ere, aspexī, aspectum: to see
attonitus, -a, -um: astonished, stunned
contrā: against (*prep. + acc.*); on the other hand, opposite (*adv.*)
damnō (1): to condemn
decōrus, -a, -um: seemly, handsome, fine
dēfricō, -āre, -uī, -ātum : to rub down
etiam: also, even, besides
ex(s)poliō, -īre, -īvī, -ītum: to strip naked
faūtor, -ōris m.: favorer, supporter

ferō, ferre, tulī, lātum: to carry, bear, endure
foedus, -a, -um: foul, ugly
ingēns, ingentis: huge, immense
masculus, -a, -um: male, masculine; a male
mīror, -ārī, -ātus sum: to wonder, be amazed
oleum, -ī n.: oil, olive oil
quīdam, quaedam, quiddam: a certain (person or thing)
quōmodo: as, in the way that (*adv.*)
soleō, -ēre, -itus sum: to be accustomed, to usually (do something)
speciēs, -ēī f.: appearance
volūtō (1): to roll, twist

---

populum ingentem attonitum: *a huge crowd, stunned;* this meaning of *populus* is frequent in the *Passiō*
quod nōn mitterentur mihi bēstiae: *because the beasts were not sent to me;* there is no clear reason for the subjunctive (see Introduction VI.G)
contrā mē: *against me;* here *contrā* is a preposition
Aegyptius foedus speciē: *an Egyptian, ugly in appearance;* the *speciē* is abl. of description
pugnātūrus mēcum: *in order to fight with me;* future participle expressing purpose
facta sum masculus: *I became a man;* the verb agrees with its feminine subject (Perpetua), the predicate nominative is masculine (*masculus*), reflecting what Perpetua has now become
quōmodo solent (facere): *as they usually (do);* athletes would be rubbed down with oil before exercise
in agōnem: *for a fight;* here *in* + acc. means "for" with a sense of purpose
illum contrā Aegyptium: *that Egyptian, opposite (to me);* the *contrā* here is an adverb
in afā volūtantem: *rolling in the sand;* wrestlers would be sprinkled with a light dust in order to be able to grip each other better

8. Et exīvit vir quīdam mīrae magnitūdinis ut etiam excēderet fastīgium amphitheātrī, discīnctātus, purpuram inter duōs clāvōs per medium pectus habēns, et galliculās multifōrmēs ex aurō et argentō factās, efferēns virgam quasi lanista, et rāmum viridem in quō erant māla aurea. 9. Et petiit silentium et dīxit, "Hic Aegyptius, sī hanc vīcerit, occīdet illam gladiō; haec, sī hunc vīcerit, accipiet rāmum istum." 10. Et recessit.

---

amphitheātrum, -ī n.: amphitheater, arena
argentum, -ī n.: silver
aureus, -a, -um: golden
aurum, -ī n.: gold
clāvus, -ī m.: nail; stripe
discingō, -ere, discīnxī, discīnctum (discīnctātum): to unbelt, loosen
duo, duae, duo: two
efferō, efferre, extulī, ēlātum: to carry out; raise up
excēdō, -ere, excessī, excessum: to exceed, go beyond
fastīgium, -iī n.: top, roof
gallicula, -ae f.: Gallic shoe, sandal
lanista, -ae m.: trainer (of gladiators)
magnitūdō, -tūdinis f.: magnitude, size

mālum, -ī n.: apple
mīrus, -a, -um: marvelous
multifōrmis, -e: many-shaped, intricate
occīdō, -ere, occīdī, occīsus: to kill, cut down
ōsculor, -ārī, -ātus sum: to kiss
pectus, pectoris n.: breast, chest
purpura, -ae f.: crimson, purple
rāmus, -ī m.: branch
recēdō, -ere, recessī, recessum: to go back, withdraw
silentium, -iī n.: silence
vincō, -ere, vīcī, victum: to conquer, defeat
virga, -ae f.: rod
viridis, -e: green

---

mīrae magnitūdinis: *of such a marvelous size;* genitive of description modifying *vir quīdam*
ut … amphitheātrī: *such that he even exceeded (the height of) the top of the amphitheater;* result clause
pupuram (tunicam) … per medium pectus habēns: *having a tunic (that was) purple between two stripes through the middle of the chest;* this is a difficult clause whose meaning is disputed
et galliculās: *and sandals;* like the *purpuram (tunicam)*, the sandals are the direct object of *habēns;* the tall man is wearing both a purple tunic and strappy sandals
purpuram (tunicam) … habēns, et galliculās: *habēns* takes *pupuram (tunicam)* and *galliculās* as objects; the tall man is wearing both a purple tunic and strappy sandals
efferēns: *holding up;* the participle *efferēns* (like *habēns*) is modifying the man; it takes *virgam* and *rāmum* as direct objects; the tall man is carrying both a rod and a branch
māla aurea: *golden apples;* perhaps a reference to the apples won by Hercules from the garden of the Hesperides, a kind of mythic paradise

Et accessimus ad invicem et coepimus mittere pugnōs. Ille mihi pedēs apprehendere volēbat; ego autem illī calcibus faciem caedēbam. 11. Et sublāta sum in āere et coepī eum sīc caedere quasi terram nōn calcāns. At ubi vīdī moram fierī, iūnxī manūs ut digitōs in digitōs mitterem et apprehendī illī caput; et cecidit in faciem et calcāvī illī caput. 12. Et coepit populus clāmāre et faūtōrēs meī psallere. Et accessī ad lanistam et accēpī rāmum. 13. Et ōsculātus est mē et dīxit mihi: "Fīlia, pāx tēcum." Et coepī īre cum glōriā ad portam Sanavivāriam.

Et experrēcta sum. 14. Et intellēxī mē nōn ad bēstiās, sed contrā Diabolum esse pugnātūram; sed sciēbam mihi esse victōriam. 15. Hoc ūsque in prīdiē mūneris ēgī; ipsīus autem mūneris āctum, sī quis voluerit, scrībat.

āēs, āeris m.: air
cadō, cadere, cecidī, cāsum: to fall
caedō, -ere, cecīdī, caesum: to cut; strike
calx, calcis f.: heel
clāmō (1): to shout, cry out
contrā: against, opposite, facing (+ acc.)
Diabolus, -ī m.: Satan (Grk. Slanderer)
digitus, -ī m.: finger
faūtor, -ōris m.: favorer, supporter
iungō, -ere, iūnxī, iūnctum: to join, attach
lanista, -ae m.: trainer (of gladiators)

mora, -ae f.: delay, hesitation
pāx, pācis f.: peace
prīdiē: on the day before, the previous day
psallō, -ere, psallī: to sing; sing a hymn
pugnus, -ī m.: a fist
rāmus, -ī m.: branch
Sanavivāria, -ae f.: "Safe-Alive," the gate through which surviving gladiators could exit
scrībō, -ere, scrīpsī, scrīptum: to write
tollō, -ere, sustulī, sublātum: to raise
victōria, -ae f.: victory

---

ad invicem: *to each other;* here *invicem* is used as a reflexive pronoun
mittere pugnōs: *throw punches*
illī calcibus faciem caedēbam: *I was striking his face with my heels;* here *illī* is dative with *faciem,* a common way to show possession of body parts
sublāta sum in āere: *I was raised into the air;* here *in* + abl. indicates motion towards rather than static location (see Introduction VI.B); *sublāta sum* is from *tollō, -ere, sustulī, sublātum* ("to raise")
Fīlia, pāx (sit) tēcum: *Daughter, peace be with you;* on the "Kiss of Peace," see Introduction V.A
Et experrēcta sum. Et intellēxī: *And I woke. And I understood;* the standard way in this narrative for a vision to end (cf. 4.10, 7.9, 8.4, and 13.8)
mihi esse victōriam: *that I had the victory;* lit. "that there was victory for me," dat. of possession
Hoc ūsque ... ēgī: *This (is what) I did up until the day before the games;* the word *ūsque* as a preposition is sometimes preceded by its acc. object (here *Hoc*)
āctum: *as for the action;* lit. "the thing done"; Perpetua cannot write the account of her own death so she leaves it to whoever wishes to do so

Perpetua's narrative has ended. The Redactor now introduces the narrative of Satyrus: a vision of a heavenly afterlife.

11.1 Sed et Satūrus benedictus hanc vīsiōnem suam ēdidit, quam ipse cōnscrīpsit.

2. Passī (inquit) erāmus, et exīvimus dē carne, et coepimus ferrī ā quattuor angelīs in orientem, quōrum manūs nōs nōn tangēbant. 3. Ībāmus autem nōn supīnī sūrsum versī, sed quasi mollem clīvum ascendentēs. 4. Et līberātō prīmō mundō vīdimus lūcem immēnsam, et dīxī Perpetuae (erat enim haec in latere meō): "Hoc est quod nōbīs Dominus prōmittēbat: percēpimus prōmissiōnem."

5. Et dum gestāmur ab ipsīs quattuor angelīs, factum est nōbīs spatium grande, quod tāle fuit quasi viridārium, arborēs habēns rosae et omne genus flōrēs.

---

arbor, -oris f.: tree
benedictus, -a, -um: blessed
clīvus, -ī m.: slope
ēdō, -ere, ēdidī, ēditum: to put forth, publish
ferō, ferre, tulī, lātum: to carry, bear, endure
flōs, -ōris m.: flower, blossom
genus, -eris n.: kind, sort
gestō (1): to carry, bear
grandis, -e: large, grand, great
latus, -eris n.: side
līberō (1): to free; to pass over
mollis, -e: soft, gentle
mundus, -ī m.: world

oriēns, orientis: east, lit. "(sōl) oriēns" ("the rising sun")
percipiō, -ere, -cēpī, -ceptum: to receive, get, take in completely
prīmus, -a, -um: first
prōmissiō, -ōnis f.: promise
prōmittō, -ere, -mīsī, -missum: to promise
supīnus, -a, -um: lying on one's back
sūrsum: upwards
tangō, -ere, tetigī, tactum: to touch
vertō, -ere, vertī, versum: to turn
viridārium, -ī n.: orchard, garden

Passī ... erāmus: from the verb *patior*, this statement can mean "we had suffered" or "we had endured"; Satyrus begins his narrative after their deaths in the arena
inquit: *he said;* the Redactor added *inquit* to mark the beginning of Satyrus's narrative
nōn supīnī sūrsum versī ... ascendentēs: *not on our backs turned upwards but as if ascending a gentle slope;* they are climbing upwards, not being carried after death
līberātō prīmō mundō: *with the first world having been passed over (by us);* abl. absolute; *līberāre* can have a sense of "to pass over"
in latere meō: *at my side*
factum est ... spatium grande: *a great space appeared;* the *spatium grande* is the neuter subject of the perfect passive verb
quod tāle fuit quasi: *which was like;* lit. "which was of such a sort as if"
omne genus flōrēs: *flowers of every sort;* the *omne genus* is a fixed idiom, which remains acc.

6. Altitūdō arborum erat in modum cypressī, quārum folia cadēbant sine cessātiōne. 7. Ibi autem in viridāriō aliī quattuor angelī fuērunt, clāriōrēs cēterīs: quī, ubi vīdērunt nōs, honōrem nōbīs dedērunt, et dīxērunt cēterīs angelīs "Ecce sunt! Ecce sunt!" cum admīrātiōne. Et expavēscentēs quattuor illī angelī quī gestābant nōs, dēposuērunt nōs. 8. Et pedibus nostrīs trānsīvimus stadium viā lātā. 9. Ibi invēnimus Iocundum et Sāturnīnum et Artaxium, quī eādem persecūtiōne vīvī ārsērunt, et Quīntum, quī et ipse martyr in carcere exierat. Et quaerēbāmus dē illīs ubi essent. 10. Cēterī angelī dīxērunt nōbīs: "Venīte prius, introīte et salūtāte Dominum."

---

admīrātiō, -tiōnis f.: admiration, wonder
altitūdō, -tūdinis f.: height
arbor, -oris f.: tree
ārdeō, -ēre, ārsī, ārsum: to burn
Artaxius, -ī m.: Artaxius
cadō, cadere, cecidī, cāsum: to fall
cessātiō, -tiōnis f.: cessation; cease
clārus, -a, -um: bright; glorious
cypressus, -ī f.: cypress tree
dēpōnō, -ere, -posuī, -positum: to put down
dum: while, as long as, until
ecce: behold!, look!
expavēscō, -ere, expāvī: to fear greatly, be terrified
folium, -ī n.: leaf, foliage
gestō (1): to carry, bear

grandis, -e: large, grand, great
honor, -ōris m.: honor, glory
inveniō, -īre, -vēnī, -ventum: to find
Iocundus, -ī m.: Jocundus
lātus, -a, -um: wide, broad
lūx, lūcis f.: light
modus, -ī m.: way, manner; measure
persecūtiō, -tiōnis f.: prosecution, persecution
quaerō, -ere, -sīvī, -sītum: to ask, inquire
Quīntus, -ī m.: Quintus
salūtō (1): to greet
Sāturnīnus, -ī m.: Saturninus
stadium, -iī n.: stadium; large open area
trānseō, -īre, -iī (-īvī), -itum: to go across
vīvus, -a, -um: alive, living

---

clāriōrēs cēterīs: *brighter than the others;* the word *clāriōrēs* is a comparative adjective with the abl. of comparison *cēterīs*
quī: *and these;* lit. "which (angels)"; a connecting relative whose antecedent is the four other angels
Ecce sunt (hīc)!: *Look, they are here!*
pedibus nostrīs: *on foot;* abl. of means
viā lātā: *by a broad path;* abl. of means
Iocundum et Sāturnīnum et Artaxium ... et Quīntum: we have no information about these figures except what Satyrus writes here
eādem persecūtiōne: *in the same persecution;* abl. of time when
quaerēbāmus dē illīs ubi essent: *we asked them where they were;* lit. "we asked from them where they themselves were"; this is an indirect question
Venīte ... introīte et salūtāte: *Come ... enter and greet;* plural imperatives

Satyrus's vision continues: a meeting with God.

12.1 Et vēnimus prope locum, cuius locī parietēs tālēs erant quasi dē lūce aedificātī; et ante ōstium locī illīus angelī quattuor stābant, quī introeuntēs vestiērunt stolās candidās. 2. Et introīvimus, et audīvimus vōcem ūnītam dīcentem "Agios agios agios" sine cessātiōne. 3. Et vīdimus in eōdem locō sedentem quasi hominem cānum, niveōs habentem capillōs et vultū iuvenīlī, cuius pedēs nōn vīdimus. 4. Et in dextrā et in sinistrā seniōrēs quattuor, et post illōs cēterī seniōrēs complūrēs stābant. 5. Et introeuntēs cum admīrātiōne stetimus ante thronum, et quattuor angelī sublevāvērunt nōs et ōsculātī sumus illum,

---

admīrātiō, -tiōnis f.: admiration, wonder
aedificō (1): to build
candidus, -a, -um: bright white
capillus, -ī m.: hair
cessātiō, -tiōnis f.: cessation, cease
complūrēs, -plūra: very many
dexter, -tra, -trum: right, the right side
gestō (1): to carry, bear, wear
iuvenīlis, -e: youthful
lūx, lūcis f.: light
niveus, -a, -um: snowy, snow white
ōsculor, -ārī, -ātus sum: to kiss

ōstium, -iī n.: entrance, opening; door
pariēs, -etis m.: wall
prope: near (+ *acc.*)
sedeō, -ēre, sēdī, sessum: to sit
sinister, -tra, -trum: left, the left side
stola, -ae f.: stola, long upper garment, robe
sublevō (1): to lift up, raise up, support, assist
thronus, -ī m.: throne
ūnītus, -a, -um: united
vestiō, -īre, -īvī, -ītum: to clothe, dress
vōx, vōcis f.: voice; utterance, word
vultus, -ūs m.: face; expression

---

cuius locī parietēs: *whose walls;* lit. "of which place the walls"
quī introeuntēs vestiērunt stolās candidās: *who clothed those entering in bright white robes; vestiērunt* takes a double accusative here, so it has the sense of clothing someone (*introeuntēs*) in something (*stolās*)
Agios agios agios: *Holy holy holy;* "(h)agios" is Greek for "holy" (ἄγιος), in the nom./sg./masc.
quasi hominem cānum: *one like an old man;* the word *cānus* ("gray") can have a sense of "gray-haired" or "old"
vultū iuvenīlī: *with a young face;* abl. of description
in dextrā (manū) et in sinistrā (manū): *on the right-hand side and on the left-hand side;* both *dextrā* and *sinistrā* are feminine because there is an implied *manū* with each, and *manus* is a feminine noun
(erant) seniōrēs: *there were elders;* the comparative form of the adj. *senex* ("old") used substantively

et dē manū suā trāiēcit nōbīs in faciem.

6. Et cēterī seniōrēs dīxērunt nōbīs: "Stēmus."

Et stetimus et pācem fēcimus.

Et dīxērunt nōbīs seniōrēs: "Īte et lūdite."

7. Et dīxī Perpetuae: "Habēs quod vīs."

Et dīxit mihi: "Deō grātiās, ut, quōmodo in carne hilaris fuī, hilarior sum et hīc modo."

Satyrus's vision concludes: Perpetua mediates a dispute.

13.1 Et exīvimus et vīdimus ante forēs Optātum, episcopum, ad dexteram et Aspasium, presbyterum doctōrem, ad sinistram, sēparātōs et trīstēs.

Aspasius, -ī m.: Aspasius (priest)
dexter, -tera, -terum: right, the right side
doctor, -ōris m.: instructor, teacher
episcopus, -ī m.: overseer; bishop
foris, -is f.: door, gate
hīc: here
lūdō, -ere, lūsī, lūsum: to play
Optātus, -ī m.: Optatus (bishop)

pāx, pācis f.: peace
presbyter, -erī m.: elder; priest
sēparō (1): to separate, divide
sinister, -tra, -trum: left, the left side
trāiciō, -ere, -iēcī, -iectum: to throw across, cause to go across, put over
trīstis, -e: sad, sullen

---

dē manū suā trāiēcit nōbīs in faciem: *he put his hand over our face;* lit. "with his hand he crossed over (onto) our face." This is a difficult sentence both because the Latin is unclear and the gesture obscure. The *dē manū* here is probably an abl. of means, which sometimes takes the preposition *dē* in later Latin (see Introduction VI.C); the *in* emphasizes the placing of hands on the face
Stēmus: *Let us stand (still);* jussive subjunctive
pācem fēcimus: *we kissed;* lit. "we made peace"; this is the ritual "kiss of peace" (see Introduction V.A)
Īte et lūdite: *Go and play;* plural imperative; this command may order a return to childlike innocence in the same way that Dinocrates played in Perpetua's earlier vision. Alternatively, *lūdite* here may have a sense of "to be carefree"
Deō grātiās (agō): *Thanks to God*
ut ... hilarior sum et hīc modo: *because ... I am more cheerful even here now;* the *ut* here is "because," so *sum* is in the indicative
ad dexteram (manum) ... ad sinistram (manum): *toward the right-hand side ... toward the left-hand side;* the *dexteram* and *sinistram* are both feminine because of the implied *manum*
Aspasium, presbyterum (et) doctōrem: *Aspasius, the priest and teacher*

2. Et mīsērunt sē ad pedēs nōbīs et dīxērunt: "Compōnite inter nōs, quia exīstis, et sīc nōs relīquistis."

3. Et dīximus illīs: "Nōn tū es pāpa noster et tū presbyter, ut vōs ad pedēs nōbīs mittātis?" Et mōtī sumus et complexī illōs sumus.

4. Et coepit Perpetua Graecē cum illīs loquī, et sēgregāvimus eōs in viridārium sub arbore rosae. 5. Et dum loquimur cum eīs, dīxērunt illīs angelī: "Sinite illōs refrīgerent; et sī quās habētis inter vōs dissēnsiōnēs, dīmittite vōbīs invicem." 6. Et conturbāvērunt eōs.

Et dīxērunt Optātō: "Corrige plēbem tuam, quia sīc ad tē conveniunt quasi dē circō redeuntēs et dē factiōnibus certantēs."

---

arbor, -oris f.: tree
certō (1): to fight
circus, -ī m.: circle; chariot racetrack
complector, -ī, complexus sum: to embrace
compōnō, -ere, -posuī, -positum: to put together; end strife, reconcile
conturbō (1): to confound; rebuke
conveniō, -īre, -vēnī, -ventum: to come together, convene, assemble
corrigō, -ere, -rēxī, -rectum: to straighten out, correct
dīmittō, -ere, -mīsī, -missum: to send away; let go, forgive
dissēnsiō, -ōnis f.: disagreement, dissension

dum: while
factiō, factiōnis f.: faction; charioteer team
Graecē: in Greek
loquor, -ī, locūtus sum: to speak, say
moveō, movēre, mōvī, mōtum: to move, rouse
Optātus, -ī m.: Optatus (bishop)
pāpa, -ae m.: father, papa; bishop
plēbs, plēbis f.: common people; crowd
redeō, -īre, -īvī, -itum: to go back, return
rosa, -ae f.: rose
sēgregō (1): to set apart, separate
sinō, -ere, sīvī, situm: to allow, let, permit
sub: under, below, beneath, underneath
viridārium, -ī n.: orchard, garden

Nōn tū es pāpa noster et tū presbyter (noster): *Are you not our bishop and you our priest;* they address Optatus and Aspasius each individually

(quaerimus) ut vōs ad pedēs nōbīs mittātis: *(we ask) how could you throw yourselves at our feet;* this is an indirect question set up by an implied verb of questioning; *ut* means "how" here

Sinite illōs refrīgerent: *Let them rest;* lit. "Allow them (that) they be refreshed"; *sinere* can take either an infinitive complement or (as here) a subjunctive; *refrīgerāre* can have an active sense ("to refresh") or a passive sense ("to be refreshed")

sī quās habētis inter vōs dissēnsiōnēs, dīmittite vōbīs invicem: *if you have any disagreements between you, forgive each other for your own sakes;* the *quās* is in place of *aliquās*, as usual after *sī, nisi, num,* or *nē, dīmittite* is an imperative, *vōbīs* is a dat. of advantage, and *invicem* a reflexive pronoun ("each other")

dē factiōnibus certantēs: *fighting over teams;* the sense is that they are clashing like rowdy sports fans

7. Et sīc nōbīs vīsum est quasi vellent claudere portās. 8. Et coepimus illīc multōs frātrēs cognōscere, sed et martyrās. Ūniversī odōre inēnārrābilī alēbāmur quī nōs satiābat.

Tunc gaudēns experrēctus sum.

The Redactor concludes the visions of Perpetua and Satyrus, then notes the death of a martyr who died in prison.

14.1 Hae vīsiōnēs īnsigniōrēs ipsōrum martyrum beātissimōrum Saturī et Perpetuae, quās ipsī cōnscrīpsērunt. 2. Secundulum vērō Deus mātūriōre exitū dē saeculō adhūc in carcere ēvocāvit nōn sine grātiā ut bēstiās lucrārētur. 3. Gladium tamen etsī nōn anima certē carō eius agnōvit.

---

agnōscō, -ere, -nōvī, -nitum: to recognize
alō, -ere, aluī, altum/alitum: to nourish, feed
anima, -ae f.: breath, soul, life
beātus, -a, -um: blessed, happy
certē: certainly
claudō, -ere, clausī, clausum: to close, shut off
etsī: even if, although, though
ēvocō (1): to call out, summon
exitus, -ūs m.: death

illīc: there, in that place
inēnārrābilis, -e: indescribable
īnsignis, -e: extraordinary, remarkable
lucror, -ārī, lucrātus sum: to gain, win, make
mātūrus, -a , -um: early, timely
odor, -ōris m.: scent, smell, odor; perfume
satiō (1): to fill, satisfy
Secundulus, -ī m.: Secundulus
vērō: but; and (postpositive)

---

vīsum est: *it seemed;* the verb *vidēre* in the passive can be "to seem"
frātrēs: *brothers;* that is, fellow Christians
Ūniversī (nōs) odōre inēnārrābilī alēbāmur: *We were all nourished by an indescribable odor*
experrēctus sum: *I awoke;* the usual expression for ending a vision in the *Passiō* (cf. 4.10, 7.9, 8.4, 10.13)
Hae (erant) vīsiōnēs īnsigniōrēs: *these (were) the quite remarkable visions;* the word *īnsigniōrēs* is the comparative form of *īnsignis*, here with a sense of "very" rather than "more"
mātūriōre exitū: *by an early death;* abl. of means
dē saeculō: *from this world;* the word *saeculum* here meaning "this present world," as often in early Christian texts, rather than "age"
adhūc in carcere: *(while) still in prison;* these words to be taken together
ut … lucrārētur: *so that he might gain by escaping the beasts;* the verb *lucrārī* can have a sense of "to gain through avoiding/escaping (something)"
Gladium tamen etsī nōn anima certē carō eius agnōvit: *Nevertheless his flesh if not his spirit knew the sword;* the language here is clear but the meaning obscure; there seems to be a reference to Luke 2:35 ("and a sword will pierce your own soul too")

The Redactor describes the labor of Felicity.

15.1 Circā Fēlīcitātem vērō et illī grātia dominī eiusmodī contigit. 2. Cum octō iam mēnsium ventrem habēret (nam praegnāns fuerat apprehēnsa), īnstante spectāculī diē, in magnō erat lūctū nē propter ventrem differrētur (quia nōn licet praegnantēs poenae repraesentārī) et nē inter aliōs posteā scelerātōs sānctum et innocentem sanguinem funderet. 3. Sed et conmartyrēs graviter contrīstābantur nē tam bonam sociam quasi comitem sōlam in viā eiusdem speī relinquerent.

---

circā: about; in regard to
comes, -itis m./f.: companion, comrade
conmartyr, -martyris m./f.: fellow martyr
contingō, -ere, -tigī, -tāctum: to happen (+ *dat.*)
contrīstō (1): to sadden, cast gloom over
differō, differre, distulī, dīlātum: to differ; delay
eiusmodī: in such manner, of such kind (*adv.*)
graviter: heavily, severely, seriously
innocēns, -entis: innocent; harmless
īnstō, -āre, -stitī, -stātum: to stand on; draw near
licet, -ēre, -uit, -itum: to be allowed, permitted
lūctus, -ūs m.: grief, distress, anxiety
mēnsis, -is m.: month

nam: for, because
octō: eight
poena, -ae f.: punishment, penalty
posteā: thereafter, afterwards
praegnāns, -antis: pregnant
repraesentō (1): to show, exhibit, display
scelerātus, -a, -um: wicked, criminal
socius, -ī m.: comrade, ally, companion
sōlus, -a, -um: alone, lone, sole
spectāculum, -ī n.: spectacle, game, show
tam: so, so much, so very, such
venter, ventris m.: belly; womb
vērō: but; and (postpositive)

---

et illī: *even to her;* that is, to Felicity
octō iam mēnsium: *of eight months;* gen. of description
fuerat apprehēnsa: *she had been arrested;* = erat apprehēnsa (on the form see Introduction VI.F)
in magnō erat lūctū: *she was in (a state of) great anxiety (fearing);* this phrase sets up two fear clauses: nē ... differrētur and nē ... funderet
nē ... differrētur: *(fearing) that (her execution) would be delayed;* pregnant women could not be executed, so she feared she would not be martyred alongside her fellow Christians
nōn licet ... repraesentārī: *it is not allowed that pregnant women be put on show for their punishment;* that is, they cannot be executed
poenae: *for punishment;* dat. of purpose
nē ... funderet: *(fearing) that she would pour out;* another fear clause, coordinated with nē ... differrētur and set up by in magnō ... lūctū
contrīstābantur nē ... reliquerent: *were saddened, (fearing) that they would leave behind;* fear clause
in viā eiusdem speī: *on the road to the same hope;* that is, martyrdom

4. Coniūnctō itaque ūnītō gemitū ad Dominum ōrātiōnem fūdērunt ante tertium diem mūneris. 5. Statim post ōrātiōnem dolōrēs invāsērunt. Et cum prō nātūrālī difficultāte octāvī mēnsis in partū labōrāns dolēret, ait illī quīdam ex ministrīs cataractāriōrum: "Quae sīc modo dolēs, quid faciēs obiecta bēstiīs, quās contempsistī cum sacrificāre nōluistī?"

6. Et illa respondit: "Modo ego patior quod patior; illīc autem alius erit in mē quī patiētur prō mē, quia et ego prō illō passūra sum." 7. Ita ēnīxa est puellam, quam sibi quaedam soror in filiam ēducāvit.

āiō: to say, affirm (ait 3rd/sg./pres.)
cataractārius, -ī m.: prison guard
coniungō, -ere, -iūnxī, -iūnctum: to join
contemnō, -ere, -psī, -ptum: to look down on
difficultās, -tātis f.: difficulty
doleō, -ēre, -uī, -itum: to feel pain, suffer
ēducō (1): to bring up, rear, foster
ēnītor, -ī, ēnīxus sum: to struggle; give birth
ergō: therefore, consequently
fundō, -ere, fūdī, fūsum: to pour (out)
gemitus, -ūs m.: groan, sigh
illīc: there, in that place
invādō, -ere, -vāsī, -vāsum: to enter, go into
labōrō (1): to labor; struggle; suffer
mēnsis, -is m.: month

minister, -trī m.: servant, attendant
modo: now (*adv.*)
nātūrālis, -e: of birth; natural
obiciō, -ere, -iēcī, -iectum: to throw at or to
octāvus, -a, -um: eighth
ōrātiō, -ōnis f.: a speech; prayer
partus, -ūs m.: birth, giving birth
patior, patī, passus sum: to suffer; endure
quīdam, quaedam, quiddam: a certain (person or thing)
sacrificō (1): to sacrifice, perform sacrifice
statim: immediately
tertius, -a, -um: third
ūnītus, -a, -um: single, united

---

ante tertium diem mūneris: *two days before the games;* lit. "before the third day"; Romans counted inclusively when counting days, so "two days" is the "third day" from the one on which counting begins
dolōrēs: *(labor) pains*
ait illī: *said to her;* referring to Felicity
Quae sīc modo dolēs: *since you suffer so much now;* lit. "you who suffer in such a way now"
obiecta: *when you have been thrown;* nom./fem./sg. of the perfect passive participle of *obicere*, acting as the subject of *faciēs*
cum sacrificāre nōluistī: *when you were unwilling to sacrifice;* temporal *cum* clause; Felicity could have been spared if she had sacrificed to the emperors (cf. 6.3)
Modo ... illīc: *now ... there (in the arena)*
in filiam ēducāvit: *raised as a daughter*

The Redactor tells a story of Perpetua's confrontation with a jailer.

16.1 Quoniam ergō permīsit et permittendō voluit Spīritus Sānctus ōrdinem ipsīus mūneris cōnscrībī, etsī indignī ad supplēmentum tantae glōriae dēscrībendae, tamen quasi mandātum sānctissimae Perpetuae, immō fideīcommissum eius exsequimur, ūnum adicientēs documentum dē ipsīus cōnstantiā et animī sublīmitāte. 2. Cum ā tribūnō castīgātius eō tractantur, quia ex admonitiōnibus hominum vānissimōrum verēbātur nē subtraherentur dē carcere incantātiōnibus aliquibus magicīs, in faciem eī Perpetua respondit:

---

adiciō, -ere, -iēcī, -iectum: to add
admonitiō, -ōnis f.: warning, admonition
animus, -ī m.: mind, spirit
castīgātius: more/very strictly (*comp. adv.*)
cōnstantia, -ae f.: perseverance, resolve
dēscrībō, -ere, -scrīpsī, -ptum: to describe
documentum, -ī n.: example; proof
eō: for this reason (*adv.*)
etsī: even if, although, though
exsequor, exsequī, exsecūtus sum: to carry out; execute
fideīcommissum, -ī n.: a bequest (in a will)
illō: there, to that place (*adv.*)
immō: in fact rather; actually
incantātiō, -tiōnis f.: enchantment

indignus, -a, -um: unworthy
magicus, -a, -um: magical
mandātum, ī n.: an order, command
ōrdō, -inis m.: order, line, series (of events)
permittō, -ere, -mīsī, -missum: to permit
quoniam: since, because
sublīmitās, -tātis f.: loftiness, elevation
subtrahō, -ere, -trāxī, -tractum: to take away secretly
supplēmentum, -ī n.: completion
tractō (1): to handle; treat
tribūnus, -ī m.: tribune
vānus, -a, -um: empty; lying, deceptive
vereor, -ērī, veritus sum: to fear

---

et permittendō voluit: *and by permitting, willed;* gerund as an abl. of means
etsī indignī: *although we are unworthy;* the *indignī* is nom./pl., *exsequimur* is the verb; the Redactor is using plural for singular, as is common in the first person
ad supplēmentum tantae glōriae dēscrībendae: *for the completion of describing such great glory;* lit. "of such great glory to be described"; as often, a gerundive phrase replaces a gerund + acc. (*dēscrībendī tantam glōriam/* "of describing such great glory")
dē ipsīus cōnstantiā: *concerning the resolve of this very woman;* referring to Perpetua
castīgātius eō tractantur, quia: *they were treated very strictly for the following reason, since;* the adverb *eō* ("for this reason") sets up the explanation in the following clause
ex admonitiōnibus hominum vānissimōrum: *because of the warnings of extremely deceptive men; ex* has the root meaning "out of" but can carry a sense of cause
nē subtraherentur: *that they would be carried off;* fear clause
in faciem eī: *to his face;* the *eī* is dative because body parts often take a dative of reference instead of a possessive adjective or genitive

3 "Quid utique nōn permittis nōbīs refrīgerāre noxiīs nōbilissimīs, Caesaris scīlicet, et nātālī eiusdem pugnātūrīs? Aut nōn tua glōria est, sī pinguiōrēs illō prōdūcāmur?" 4. Horruit et ērubuit tribūnus; et ita iussit illōs hūmānius habērī ut frātribus eius et cēterīs facultās fieret introeundī et refrīgerandī cum eīs, iam et ipsō optiōne carceris crēdente.

The Redactor describes a last supper in prison.

17.1 Prīdiē quoque cum illam cēnam ultimam, quam "līberam" vocant, quantum in ipsīs erat, nōn cēnam līberam sed agapēn cēnārent,

---

agapē, -is f.: love; the Feast of Love
animus, -ī m.: mind, spirit
Caesar, -aris m.: Caesar
cēna, -ae f.: dinner
cēnō (1): to dine, eat dinner
ērubēscō, -ere, ērubuī: to be red, blush
facultās, -tātis f.: ability, opportunity
horreō, -ēre, -uī: to shudder, bristle with fear
hūmānius: more humanely (*comp. adv.*)
illō: there, to that place (*adv.*)
iubeō, -ēre, iussī, iussum: to order, bid
līber, lībera, līberum: free
nātāle, -is n.: birthday (masc. in Classical Latin)

nōbilis, -e: noble, good, honorable
noxius, -a, -um: harmful; criminal
optiō, -iōnis m.: centurion's assistant
permittō, -ere, -mīsī, -missum: to permit
pinguis, -e: fat, well-fed
prīdiē: on the day before, the previous day
prōdūcō, -ere, -xī, -ductum: to lead forward
quantum: so much as, how much (*adv.*)
quoque: also
scīlicet: obviously; in particular
tribūnus, -ī m.: tribune
ultimus, -a, -um: last, final

Quid utique: *why on earth;* the word *utique* ("in any case") functions as an intensifier, as it often does in the *Passiō*
nōbīs refrīgerāre noxiīs nōbilissimīs: *us, the most honorable criminals, to get refreshment;* the *nōbīs* is dative with *permittis*, and *noxiīs nōbilissimīs* agrees with *nōbīs*; the verb *refrīgerāre* can have a passive sense ("to be refreshed")
Caesaris scīlicet: *of Caesar, no less;* the word *scīlicet* can have an emphatic sense in enumeration, like English "in particular" or "no less"
nātālī eiusdem: *on his birthday;* lit. "on the birthday" (abl. of time when) "of the same person"
pugnātūrīs: *about to fight;* agrees with *nōbīs*
ut ... fieret: result clause
iam et ipsō optiōne carceris crēdente: *now with even the warden himself of the prison being a believer;* the *optiō* here is Pudens from 9.1; the verb *crēdere* has a sense of "to believe (in Christianity)" (cf. 1.5)
quam "līberam" vocant: *which they call the "free" (meal);* the final meal given to prisoners and gladiators
quantum in ipsīs erat: *as much as they could;* lit. "as much as it was in them"
agapēn cēnārent: *they ate a (feast of) love;* the Greek form of the acc. is *-ēn* rather than *-em;* the Feast of Love was an early Christian ritual (see Introduction V.A)

eādem cōnstantiā ad populum verba iactābant, comminantēs iūdicium Deī, contestantēs passiōnis suae fēlīcitātem, inrīdentēs concurrentium cūriōsitātem, dīcente Saturō: 2. "Crastinus satis vōbīs nōn est? Quid libenter vidētis quod ōdistis? Hodiē amīcī, crās inimīcī. Notāte tamen vōbīs faciēs nostrās dīligenter, ut recognōscātis nōs in diē illō."

3. Ita omnēs inde attonitī discēdēbant, ex quibus multī crēdidērunt.

The Redactor recounts the entrance into the arena: Perpetua convinces the tribune not to force them to wear costumes.

18.1 Illūxit diēs victōriae illōrum, et prōcessērunt dē carcere in amphitheātrum quasi in caelum hilarēs, vultū decōrī, sī forte gaudiō paventēs nōn timōre.

---

amphitheātrum, -ī n.: amphitheater, arena
attonitus, -a, -um: astonished, stunned
comminor, -ārī, -ātus sum: to threaten
concurrō, -ere, -currī, -cursus: to assemble
cōnstantia, -ae f.: resolve; steadfastness
contestor, -ārī, -ātus sum: to attest
crās: tomorrow
crastinus, -a, -um: (of) tomorrow
cūriōsitās, -tātis f.: curiosity
decōrus, -a, -um: handsome; radiant
dīligenter: carefully, diligently
discēdō, -ere, -cessī, -cessum: to go away
forte: by chance (*adv.*)
gaudium, -iī n.: gladness, joy
hodiē: today, this day
iactō (1): to throw, hurl, cast

illūcescō, -ere, illūxī: to dawn
inde: from there, then, afterward
inimīcus, -a, -um: unfriendly, hostile; enemy
inrīdeō, -ēre, -rīsī, -rīsum: to laugh at, mock
iūdicium, -ī n.: judgment
libenter: gladly, willingly, with pleasure
notō (1): to note, mark
ōdī, odisse: to hate (perf. with pres. sense)
paveō, -ēre, pāvī: to tremble
prōcēdō, -ere, -cessī, -cessum: to proceed
recognōscō, -ere, -nōvī, -nitum: to recognize
satis: enough, sufficient
timor, -ōris m.: fear, dread, anxiety
victōria, -ae f.: victory
vultus, -ūs m.: face; expression

---

verba iactābant: *they were shouting;* lit. "throwing words"
comminantēs ... contestantēs ... inrīdentēs: *threatening ... attesting ... mocking;* these participles agree with the implied subject of *iactābant*
Crastinus (diēs): *Tomorrow;* lit. "Tomorrow's day"
Quid libenter vidētis: *Why do you enjoy looking at*
in diē illō: *on that day;* perhaps referring both to the day of spectacle and the day of judgement
ex quibus multī: *many of whom;* lit. "from whom, many" referring to the crowd
crēdidērunt: *have believed;* that is, have become believers in Christianity (cf. 1.5, 16.4)
vultū decōrī: *with a radiant expression;* lit. "radiant in respect to their face(s)"
sī forte gaudiō paventēs nōn timōre: *if, by chance, trembling, it was from joy, not fear*

2. Sequēbātur Perpetua lūcidō vultū et placidō incessū, ut mātrōna Christī, ut Deī dēlicāta, vigōre oculōrum dēiciēns omnium cōnspectum. 3. Item Fēlīcitās, salvam sē peperisse gaudēns ut ad bēstiās pugnāret, ā sanguine ad sanguinem, ab obstetrīce ad rētiārium, lōtūra post partum baptismō secundō. 4. Et cum ductī essent in portam et cōgerentur habitum induere, virī quidem sacerdōtum Sāturnī, fēminae vērō sacrātārum Cererī, generōsa illa in finem ūsque cōnstantiā repugnāvit.

---

baptismum, -ī n.: immersion; baptism
Cerēs, Cereris f.: Ceres (goddess)
cōgō, cōgere, coēgī, coāctum: to force
cōnspectus, -ūs m.: sight; glance, gaze
cōnstantia, -ae f.: perseverance, resolve, grit
dēlicāta, -ae f.: darling; favorite
fīnis, -is m./f.: end
generōsus, -a, -um: noble, dignified
habitus, -ūs m.: dress, attire
incessus, -ūs m.: gait, walk (incēdō)
induō, -ere, induī, indūtum: to put on
item: also, likewise, in like manner
lavō, -āre, lāvī, lōtum (lautum): to wash, bathe
lūcidus, -a, -um: clear, bright, shining
mātrōna, -ae f.: married woman, wife
obstetrīx, -īcis f.: midwife
oculus, -ī m.: eye

pariō, -ere, peperī, partum: to give birth, bear
partus, -ūs m.: birth, giving birth
placidus, -a, -um: peaceful, calm, placid
quidem: indeed, in fact, certainly
repugnō (1): to fight against; oppose, resist
rētiārius, -ī m.: net-fighting gladiator
sacerdōs, -dōtis m./f.: priest(ess)
sacrātus, -a, -um: consecrated, sacred
salvus, -a, -um: safe
sanguis, -inis m.: blood
Sāturnus, -ī m.: Saturn (god)
sequor, sequī, secūtus sum: to follow
ūsque: continuously (*adv.*)
vērō: and; but (postpositive)
vigor, -ōris m.: liveliness, strength, force
vultus, -ūs m.: face; expression

---

ut mātrōna Christī, ut Deī dēlicāta: *like a wife of Christ, like a darling of God;* here *ut* means "like"
vigōre oculōrum dēiciēns omnium cōnspectum: *the strength of her gaze caused everyone to look away;* lit. "with the strength of her eyes, throwing down the sight of all"
salvam sē peperisse: *that she had given birth safely;* lit. "that she, safe, had given birth"; this is an indirect statement governed by *gaudēns* ("rejoicing")
lōtūra (sē): *about to wash (herself);* future active participle
virī quidem sacerdōtum Sāturnī, fēminae vērō sacrātārum Cererī: *the men (were forced to put on the garb) of priests of Saturn, and the women that of women consecrated to Ceres;* these costumes would have been humiliating to Perpetua and the others who were dying specifically to avoid the worship of those gods; in Africa, Saturn was identified not only with the Greek Cronus but with the Punic Baal Hammon, and Ceres not only with the Greek Demeter but with the Punic Tanit
generōsa illa: *that noble woman;* i.e. Perpetua
cōnstantiā: *with grit;* the abl. of manner here lacks the usual preposition (*cum*)

5. Dīcēbat enim, "Ideō ad hoc sponte pervēnimus, nē lībertās nostra obdūcerētur; ideō animam nostram addīximus, nē tale aliquid facerēmus; hoc vōbīscum pactī sumus." 6. Agnōvit iniūstitia iūstitiam: concessit tribūnus. Quōmodo erant, simpliciter indūcerentur.

7. Perpetua psallēbat, caput iam Aegyptiī calcāns. Revocātus et Sāturnīnus et Satūrus populō spectantī comminābantur. 8. Dehinc ut sub cōnspectū Hilariānī pervēnērunt, gestū et nūtū coepērunt Hilariānō dīcere "Tū nōs" inquiunt, "tē autem Deus." 9. Ad hoc populus exasperātus flagellīs eōs vexārī per ōrdinem vēnātōrum postulāvit;

---

addīcō, -ere, -dīxī, -dictum: to yield, give up
agnōscō, -ere, -nōvī, -nitum: to recognize
anima, -ae f.: breath, life
comminor, -ārī, -ātus sum: to threaten (+ *dat.*)
concēdō, -ere, -cessī, -cessum: to yield, allow
cōnspectus, -ūs m.: sight, view
dehinc: from here; then, next
exasperō (1): to provoke, incite
flagellum, -ī n.: whip, scourge
gestus, -ūs m.: gesture, posture, attitude
indūcō, -ere, -dūxī, -ductum: to lead or bring in
iniūstitia, -ae f.: injustice
iūstitia, -ae f.: justice, fairness, equity

lībertās, -tātis f.: freedom, liberty
nūtus, -ūs m.: a nod, nodding
obdūcō, -ere, -dūxī, -ductum: to cover; infringe
ōrdō, -inis m.: order, line
pacīscor, pacīscī, pactus sum: agree on/to
psallō, -ere: to sing; sing a hymn
simpliciter: simply, plainly, directly
spectō (1): to watch, look at
sponte: willingly, voluntarily
sub: under, below, beneath, underneath
tribūnus, -ī m.: tribune
vēnātor, -ōris m.: beast-fighting gladiator
vexō (1): to shake; to torment

Ideō ... pervēnimus: *That's why we came;* the *ideō* ("for this reason") looks ahead to *nē ... obdūcerētur* ("so that our liberty not be infringed")

ideō ... addīximus: *that's why we handed over;* the *ideō* ("for this reason") here looks ahead to *nē ... facerēmus* ("so that we not have to do anything like this")

hoc vōbīscum pactī sumus: *we agreed on this with you;* the *hoc* is the direct object of *pactī sumus*

Quōmodo erant, simpliciter indūcerentur: *Just as they were, they were brought in plainly;* that is, they were allowed to go in with no costumes, just dressed as they were

Revocātus et Sāturnīnus et Satūrus: Revocatus and Saturninus were arrested with Perpetua; Satyrus, their teacher, turned himself in after their arrest

ut ... pervēnērunt: *when they arrived*

sub cōnspectū: *under the gaze;* an accusative would be expected because of the motion towards (cf. Introduction VI.B)

"Tū nōs (iūdicās) ... tē autem Deus (iūdicābit)": *"You (judge) us, but God (will judge) you";* implied is a verb of judging or condemning

Ad hoc: *In response to this;* referring to the situation of Hilarianus being threatened

flagellīs eōs vexārī: *that they be whipped;* lit. "tormented with whips"; an indirect statement set up by *postulāvit* ("demanded")

et utique grātulātī sunt quod aliquid et dē Dominicīs passiōnibus essent cōnsecūtī.

The Redactor describes the spectacle: the mauling of Saturninus, Revocatus, and Satyrus.

19.1 Sed quī dīxerat "Petite et accipiētis" (John 16:24), petentibus dederat eum exitum quem quisque dēsīderāverat. 2. Nam, sī quandō inter sē dē martyriī suī vōtō sermōcinābantur, Sāturnīnus quidem omnibus bēstiīs velle sē obicī profitēbātur, ut scīlicet glōriōsiōrem gestāret corōnam. 3. Itaque in commissiōne spectāculī ipse et Revocātus, leopardum expertī, etiam super pulpitum ab ursō vexātī sunt. 4. Satūrus autem nihil magis quam ursum abōminābātur; sed ūnō morsū leopardī cōnficī sē iam praesūmēbat.

---

abōminor, -ārī, -ātus sum: to hate; abhor
commissiō, -ōnis f.: commencement
cōnficiō, -ere, -fēcī, -fectum: to finish, kill
cōnsequor, cōnsequī, cōnsecūtus sum: to follow; imitate
corōna, -ae f.: crown (of victory)
dēsīderō (1): to long for, desire
dominicus, -a, -um: of the lord or master
etiam: besides, also, even
exitus, -ūs m.: death
experior, -perīrī, -pertus sum: to experience, try
gestō (1): to bear, wear
glōriōsus, -a, -um: glorious, renowned
grātulor, -ārī, -ātus sum: to be grateful, thank
magis: more, rather
martyrium, -iī n.: testimony; martyrdom
morsus, -ūs m.: bite

nam: for
nihil: nothing (*indeclinable*)
obiciō, -ere, -iēcī, -iectum: throw to
praesūmō, -ere, -psī, -psum: to presume; predict
profiteor, -ērī, professus sum: to declare, say
pulpitum, -ī n.: platform, staging, scaffold
quandō: ever, at any time
quidem: certainly, actually
quisque, quaeque, quodque: each (person or thing)
scīlicet: evidently, clearly
sermōcinor, -ārī, -ātus sum: to converse, talk
spectāculum, -ī n.: spectacle, game, show
ursus, -ī m.: a bear
vexō (1): to shake; to torment
vōtum, -ī n.: vow; desire

---

quod aliquid et dē Dominicīs passiōnibus essent cōnsecūtī: *because they had obtained some portion of the Lord's suffering too;* a reference to Jesus being whipped before crucifixion
(is) quī dīxerat: *(he) who said;* that is, Jesus
sī quandō: *if ever*
corōnam: a crown was a usual prize in athletic competitions, and early Christians used the word to describe martyrdom as a victory

5. Itaque cum aprō subministrārētur, vēnātor potius (quī illum aprō subligāverat subfossus ab eādem bēstiā) post diem mūneris obiit; Satūrus sōlummodo tractus est. 6. Et cum ad ursum substrictus esset in ponte, ursus dē caveā prōdīre nōluit. Itaque secundō Satūrus inlaesus revocātur.

The Redactor describes the spectacle: the mauling of Perpetua and Felicity.

20.1 Puellīs autem ferōcissimam vaccam ideōque praeter cōnsuētūdinem comparātam Diabolus praeparāvit, sexuī eārum etiam dē bēstiā aemulātus. 2. Itaque dispoliātae et rēticulīs indūtae prōdūcēbantur. Horruit populus, alteram respiciēns puellam dēlicātam, alteram ā partū recentem stīllantibus mammīs.

---

aemulor, -ārī, -ātus sum: to rival; match (+ *dat.*)
aper, aprī m.: wild boar
cavea, -ae f.: hollow, cavity; cage, stall
comparō (1): to prepare, furnish
cōnsuētūdō, -inis f.: custom
dēlicātus, -a, -um: delicate, tender; alluring
Diabolus, -ī m.: Satan (Grk. Slanderer)
dispoliō (1): to strip (naked)
etiam: besides, also, even
ferōx, ferōcis: fierce, ferocious, wild
horreō, -ēre, -uī: to shudder
induō, -ere, induī, indūtum: to put on
inlaesus, -a, -um: unharmed, unhurt
obeō, -īre, -īvī/-iī, -itum: to die, pass (away)
partus, -ūs m.: birth, giving birth
pōns, pontis m.: a bridge, flooring
potius: rather
praeparō (1): to prepare

praeter: beyond; contrary to (+ *acc.*)
prōdeō, -īre, -īvī, -itum: to come or go forth
prōdūcō, -ere, -xī, -ductum: to lead forward
recēns, recentis: fresh, new, recent
respiciō, -ēre, -exī, -ectum: to look at; consider
rēticulum, -ī n.: small net, fishing net, net
revocō (1): to call back, recall
secundō: for a second time (*adv.*)
sexus, -ūs m.: sex (i.e. male, female)
sōlummodo: only just, merely
stīllō (1): to drop, drip, trickle
subfodiō, -ere, -fōdī, -fossum: to dig; stab, gore
subligō (1): to tie up
subministrō (1): to provide, give, supply
substringō, -ere, -nxī, -ctum: to bind up
trahō, -ere, trāxī, tractum: to drag
vacca, -ae f.: cow
vēnātor, -ōris m.: beast-fighting gladiator

---

cum aprō subministrārētur: *although he was served up for the boar;* concessive *cum* clause
vēnātor ... quī illum aprō subligāverat: *the gladiator who had tied him (Satyrus) up for the boar*
ad ursum: *for a bear*
ideōque: *and for this reason;* = ideō + -que; this phrase looks ahead to *sexuī ... aemulātus*
praeter cōnsuētūdinem: *contrary to custom*
sexuī eārum etiam dē bēstiā aemulātus: *having matched their sex even with the beast;* meaning that the cow was also female, to match Perpetua and Felicity
alteram ... alteram: *one (Perpetua) ... the other (Felicity)*

3. Ita revocātae et discīnctīs indūtae. Prior Perpetua iactāta est et concidit in lumbōs. 4. Et ubi sēdit, tunicam ā latere dīscissam ad vēlāmentum femoris redūxit pudōris potius memor quam dolōris. 5. Dehinc acū requīsītā et dispersōs capillōs īnfībulāvit; nōn enim decēbat martyram sparsīs capillīs patī, nē in suā glōriā plangere vidērētur. 6. Ita surrēxit et ēlīsam Fēlīcitātem cum vīdisset, accessit et manum eī trādidit et suscitāvit illam. Et ambae pariter stetērunt. 7. Et populī dūritiā dēvictā, revocātae sunt in portam Sanavivāriam.

---

acus, -ūs f.: pin
ambō, -ae, -ō: both
capillus, -ī m.: hair
concidō, -ere, -cīdī: to fall, fall down
decet, decēre, decuit: to be fitting, proper
dehinc: from here, then, next
dēvincō, -ere, -vīcī, -ctum: to overcome utterly
dīscindō, -ere, -dī, -cissum: to cut or tear apart
discingō, -ere, -xī, -nctum: to unbelt, loosen
dispergō, -ere, -spersī, -spersum: to mess up
dūritia, -ae f.: hardness; cruelty
ēlīdō, -ere, -līsī, -līsum: to strike down, dash
femur, femoris n.: upper leg, thigh
iactō (1): to throw
illīc: there, in that place
induō, -ere, induī, indūtum: to put on
īnfībulō (1): to fasten (with pin), clasp
latus, -eris n.: side
lumbus, -ī m.: loin, hips and buttocks

martyra, martyrae f.: martyr
memor, memoris: mindful (+ *gen.*)
pariter: equally, side by side
plangō, -ere, -nxī, -nctum: to wail; mourn
potius: rather, more, more preferably
pudor, pudōris m.: sense of shame or honor
redūcō, -ere, -dūxī, -ductum: to draw back
requīrō, -ere, -sīvī, -sītum: to ask for
revocō (1): to call back, recall
Sanavivāria, -ae f.: "Safe-Alive," the gate through which surviving gladiators could exit the arena
sedeō, -ēre, sēdī, sessum: to sit
spargō, -ere, -sī, -sum: to strew; spread out
surgō, -ere, -rēxī, -rēctum: to rise, stand up
suscitō (1): to lift up, raise
trādō, -dere, -didī, -ditum: to give, hand over
tunica, -ae f.: tunic
vēlāmentum, -ī n.: cover; covering

---

revocātae (sunt) et discīnctīs (tunicīs) indūtae (sunt): *(they were) called back and dressed in unbelted (tunics)*
tunicam ā latere dīscissam ad vēlāmentum femoris redūxit: *she pulled her tunic, which had been torn from her side, back to cover her thigh;* lit. "for the covering of her thigh"
dispersōs capillōs ... sparsīs capillīs: *her messed up hair ... with disheveled hair*
nē ... plangere vidērētur: *so that she not ... seem to mourn;* disheveled hair was a sign of mourning
ēlīsam ... vīdisset: *when she saw that Felicity had been struck down;* this is a circumstantial *cum*-clause

8. Illīc Perpetua ā quōdam tunc catēchūmenō, Rūsticō nōmine, quī eī adhaerēbat, suscepta et quasi ā somnō expergita (adeō in spīritū et in extasī fuerat) circumspicere coepit; et stupentibus omnibus ait, "Quandō" inquit, "prōdūcimur ad vaccam illam nesciōquam?" 9. Et cum audīsset quod iam ēvēnerat, nōn prius crēdidit nisi quāsdam notās vexātiōnis in corpore et habitū suō recognōvisset. 10. Exinde accersītum frātrem suum et illum catēchūmenum adlocūta est, dīcēns: "In fidē stāte et invicem omnēs dīligite, et passiōnibus nostrīs nē scandalizēminī."

---

accersō, -ere, -īvī, -ītum: to summon, send for
adeō: so greatly
adhaereō, -ēre, -esī, -esum: to cling or stick to
adloquor, -quī, -locūtum: to address
aiō, -ere, -it: to say (ait 3rd/sg./pres.)
certē: certainly
circumspiciō, -ere, -spexī, -spectum: to look around
cōnsūmō, -ere, -psī, -ptum: to consume; destroy; kill
cor, cordis n.: heart
dīligō, -ere, -lēxī, -lēctum: to love, esteem, value
ecce: behold!, look!
ēveniō, -īre, ēvēnī, ēventum: to turn out, happen
exhortor, -ārī, -tātus sum: to exhort, encourage
exinde: from there; then, next
expergō, -ere, -gī, -gitum: to awake, rouse up
extasis, -is f.: ecstasy
habitus, -ūs m.: dress, attire
illō: there, to that place (*adv.*)
item: also, likewise, in like manner
morsus, -ūs m.: bite
nesciōquī, -quae, -quod: some; whatever

nōmen, nōminis n.: name
nota, -ae f.: mark, sign
nūllus, -a, -um: none, no, no one
praedīcō, -ere, -dīxī, -dictum: to predict
praesūmō, -ere, -mpsī: to presume, predict
prōdeō, -īre, -i(v)ī, prōditum: to go out
prōdūcō, -ere, -xī, -ductum: to lead forward
Pudēns, Pudentis m.: Pudens (warden, previously seen in 9.1 and 16.4)
quandō: when
recognōscō, -ere, -nōvī, -nitum: to recognize
Rūsticus, -ī m.: Rusticus
scandalizō (1): to cause to stumble, trip up; confuse, upset
sentiō, -īre, -nsī, -sum: to perceive, feel, sense
sīcut: just as, so as
somnus, -ī m.: sleep
stupeō, -ēre, -uī: to be stunned, be astounded
summus, -a, -um: top of, highest (part of)
suscipiō, -ere, -cēpī, -ceptum: to take up, take
tōtus, -a, -um: whole, entire
vacca, -ae f.: cow
vexātiō, -ōnis f.: shaking; wounding, mauling

ā quōdam tunc catēchūmenō: *by a certain man who at that time was a catechumen;* the *tunc* suggests that Rusticus has since been initiated as a Christian
Rūsticō nōmine: *named Rusticus;* lit. "Rusticus, by name"; *Rūsticō* is abl. in apposition to *quōdam ... catēchūmenō*, while *nōmine* is an abl. of respect
quī eī adhaerēbat: *who was attached to her;* this is most likely referring to emotional attachment
suscepta ... expergita: *picked up ... awoken;* each of these nominative participles agrees with Perpetua, who is the subject of *coepit*
vaccam illam nesciōquam: *that cow or whatever;* lit. "that cow, whatever one it is"
nōn prius crēdidit nisi: *she didn't believe it before she recognized;* in post-classical Latin, *nōn prius ... nisi* is an equivalent to *nōn prius ... quam*
invicem: *each other;* the word *invicem* is here used as a reflexive pronoun, as often in this text

The Redactor describes the spectacle: last words and deaths.

21.1 Item Satūrus in aliā portā Pudentem mīlitem exhortābātur dīcēns: "Ad summam," inquit, "certē, sīcut praesūmpsī et praedīxī, nūllam ūsque adhūc bēstiam sēnsī. Et nunc dē tōtō corde crēdās: Ecce prōdeō illō, et ab ūnō morsū leopardī cōnsummor." 2. Et statim in fīne spectāculī leopardō obiectus dē ūnō morsū tantō perfūsus est sanguine, ut populus revertentī illī secundī baptismatis testimōnium reclāmāverit: "Salvum lōtum! Salvum lōtum!" 3. Plānē utique salvus erat quī hōc modō lāverat. 4. Tunc Pudentī mīlitī inquit: "Valē" inquit, "memor fideī meae; et haec tē nōn conturbent, sed cōnfirment."

5. Simulque ānsulam dē digitō eius petiit, et vulnerī suō mersam reddidit eī hērēditātem, pignus relinquēns illī et memoriam sanguinis.

ānsula, -ae f.: small ring
baptisma, -matis n.: immersion; baptism
cōnfirmō (1): to make strong, strengthen
conturbō (1): to confuse, set in confusion
digitus, -ī m.: finger
fīnis, -is m./f.: end
hērēditās, -tātis f.: inheritance, heirloom
lavō, -āre, lāvī, lōtum (lautum): to wash, bathe
memor, -ōris: mindful, remembering (+ *gen.*)
memoria, -ae f.: memory
mergō, -ere, mersī, mersum: to dip, immerse
morsus, -ūs m.: bite
obiciō, -ere, -iēcī, -iectum: to throw at or to

perfundō, -ere, -ūdī, -ūsum: to pour over, drench
pignus, pignoris n.: pledge, security
plānē: clearly, plainly, simply
Pudēns, Pudentis m.: Pudens (warden)
reclāmō (1): to shout again; shout repeatedly
reddō, -ere, -didī, -ditus: to give back, return
revertō, -ere, revertī: to turn back, return
simul: at the same time, at once
spectāculum, -ī n.: spectacle, game, show
tantō: so much, so greatly (*adv.*)
testimōnium, ī n.: witness, evidence
valē: farewell, goodbye
vulnus, -eris n.: wound

Ad summam: *in sum; in short;* lit. "to the whole," a common idiom
nūllam … bēstiam sēnsī: *I have felt (the touch of) no beast*
dē tōtō corde: *from your whole heart;* the phrase could also be an abl. of means (see Introduction VI.C)
dē ūnō morsū tantō perfūsus est: *from a single bite he was so drenched;* here *tantō* is an adverb
Salvum lōtum: *Good bath;* lit. "sound(ly) washed," a phrase bathers used for wishing each other well when leaving Roman baths
salvus … lāverat: *he who bathed in this manner was saved;* there is some word play with *salvus* here. In *Salvum lōtum* the *salvus* basically meant "good." Here it means "safe, unharmed," as in, he has achieved his salvation
vulnerī suō mersam … hērēditātem: *(the ring) having been plunged into his wound, he gave it back to him as an heirloom;* the ring is being immersed in blood as a reminder of Satyrus's sacrifice

6. Exinde iam exanimis prōsternitur cum cēterīs ad iugulātiōnem solitō locō. 7. Et cum populus illōs in mediō postulāret, ut gladiō penetrantī in eōrum corpore oculōs suōs comitēs homicīdiī adiungerent, ultrō surrēxērunt et sē quō volēbat populus trānstulērunt, ante iam ōsculātī invicem ut martyrium per sollemnia pācis cōnsummārent.

8. Cēterī quidem immōbilēs et cum silentiō ferrum recēpērunt; multō magis Satūrus, quī et prior ascenderat, prior reddidit spīritum; nam et Perpetuam sustinēbat.

---

adiungō, -ere, adiūnxī, adiūnctum: to join
comes, -itis m./f.: companion
cōnsummō (1): to complete, finish
exanimis, -e: unconscious
exinde: from there; then
ferrum, -ī n.: iron; sword
homicīdium, -iī n.: murder
immōbilis, -e: immovable, immobile
iugulātiō, -ōnis n.: slitting the throat
magis: more, rather
martyrium, -iī n.: testimony; martyrdom
medium, -ī n.: the middle, the presence of all
nam: for; because
oculus, -ī m.: eye
ōsculor, -ārī, -ātus sum: to kiss
pāx, pācis f.: peace

penetrō (1): to penetrate, pierce, enter
prōsternō, -ere, -strāvī, -strātum: to throw down
quidem: indeed, in fact, certainly
quō: where, to where (*adv.*)
recipiō, -ere, recēpī, receptum: to accept
reddō, -ere, -didī, -ditum: to give back, return
silentium, -iī n.: silence
solitus, -a, -um: accustomed, usual
sollemne, -is n.: rite, ritual
surgō, -ere, -rēxī, -rēctum: to rise, stand up
sustineō, -ēre, -uī, sustentum: to support; await
trānsferō, -ferre, -tulī, -lātum: to carry across; move
ultrō: voluntarily; of one's will

---

solitō locō: *in the usual place;* abl. of place where without a preposition; the Redactor is referring to the *spoliārium*, where the body of a gladiator would be taken to be stripped
cum populus illōs in mediō postulāret: *since the crowd was demanding that they (be killed) in the presence of all;* here *medium* is the noun "middle" with a sense of "in the midst of all"; note the non-standard *in* + abl. for motion toward (see Introduction VI.B)
ut ... adiungerent: *in order that they (the spectators) might make their eyes accomplices in the murder to the sword piercing their (the martyrs) bodies;* lit. "in order that they might join their eyes ... to the sword ... "; note the non-standard *in* + abl. (*in ... corpore*) to express motion toward (see Introduction VI.B)
ōsculātī invicem: *after kissing each other;* the *invicem* is again a reflexive pronoun
per sollemnia pācis: *through rites of peace;* on the ritual Kiss of Peace see Introduction V.A
multō magis: *in particular;* lit. "much more," "more by much," an abl. of degree of difference
Satūrus, quī ... sustinēbat: a reference to Perpetua's first vision (ch. 4.5-6)

9. Perpetua autem, ut aliquid dolōris gustāret, inter ossa compūncta exululāvit, et errantem dexteram tīrunculī gladiātōris ipsa in iugulum suum trānstulit. 10. Fortasse tanta fēmina aliter nōn potuisset occīdī, quae ab inmundō spīritū timēbātur, nisi ipsa voluisset.

11. Ō fortissimī ac beātissimī martyrēs! Ō vērē vocātī et ēlēctī in glōriam Dominī nostrī Iēsū Chrīstī! Quam quī magnificat et honōrificat et adōrat, utique et haec nōn minōra veteribus exempla in aedificātiōnem Ecclēsiae legere dēbet, ut novae quoque virtūtēs ūnum et eundem semper Spīritum Sānctum ūsque adhūc operārī testificentur, et omnipotentem Deum Patrem et Fīlium eius Iēsum Chrīstum dominum nostrum, cui est clāritās et immēnsa potestās in saecula saeculōrum. Āmēn.

---

adōrō (1): to love; to adore
aedificātiō, -ōnis f.: edification; improvement
aliter: otherwise, in another way
beātus, -a, -um: blessed, happy
clāritās, -itātis f.: brightness; glory
compungō, -ere, -pūnxī, -pūnctum: to puncture
dēbeō, -ēre, -uī, debitum: to owe; ought
dexter, -tera, -terum: right, the right hand
Ecclēsia, -ae f.: assembly; church
ēligō, -ere, -lēgī, -lēctum: to pick out, choose
errō (1): to wander
exemplum, -ī n.: example
exululō (1): to howl, scream
fortasse: perhaps
gladiātor, -ōris m.: gladiator
gustō (1): to taste
honōrificō (1): to honor
inmundus, -a, -um: impure, not clean

iugulum, -ī n.: throat
legō, -ere, lēgī, lectum: to read
magnificō (1): to esteem, respect
minor, minus: less, smaller
occīdō, -ere, occīdī, occīsum: to kill, cut down
omnipotēns, -tentis: all-powerful
operor, -ārī, -ātus sum: to work; produce, be productive
os, ossis n.: bone
potestās, -tātis f.: power
quoque: also
testificor, -ārī, -ātus sum: to testify
timeō, -ēre, timuī: to fear
tīrunculus, -ī m.: novice
trānsferō, -ferre, -tulī, -lātum: to carry across; move
vērē: truly

---

inter ossa compūncta: *during the piercing of her bones;* lit. "her bones having been pierced"
Iēsū Chrīstī: *of Jesus, the annointed one;* the *Iēsū* is gen./sg. (= Grk. Ἰησοῦ)
Quam (glōriam): *and as for this glory;* this is a connecting relative
et haec: *also these, these as well;* object of *legere*
legere dēbet: the subject of *dēbet* is the implied antecedent of the relative clause "he who … adores"
ūsque adhūc: *at all points up to now;* the Redactor is once more stating the purpose of recording Perpetua's martyrdom: to prove that the same Holy Spirit remembered in older sacred texts continues to work in the same manner
in saecula saeculōrum: *for all time;* lit. "into the ages of ages"

GLOSSARY

This glossary contains all the words that are not glossed in the running vocabulary. The words in the glossary are those that occur frequently in the text (four or more times), and words that, while infrequent in the text, are likely to be known by most students (like *puella*).

ā, ab: (away) from; by
ac: and
accēdō, -ere, -cessī, -cessum: to approach, get close; begin
accipiō, -ere, accēpī, acceptum: to receive, accept, get
ad: to, toward; near, at
adhūc: still, even now
Aegyptius, -a, -um: Egyptian
agō, agere, ēgī, āctum: to drive, lead, do, act
aliquis, -quid: some (one/thing), any (one/thing)
alius, -a, -ud: other, another, else
alter, -era, -erum: other (of two)
āmēn: amen
amīcus, -a, -um: friendly (*adj.*); friend (*substantive*)
an: whether, or (in alternative indirect questions)
angelus, -ī m.: messenger; angel
annus, -ī m.: year
ante: before, in front of (*prep.* + *acc.*)
ante: before, previously (*adv.*)
apprehendō, -ere, apprehendī, apprehēnsum: seize, grab; arrest
aqua, -ae f.: water
ascendō, -ere, ascendī, ascēnsum: ascend, go up
aspiciō, -ere, aspēxī, aspectum: look at; consider
at: but
audiō, -īre, -īvī, -ītum: to hear, listen to
aut: or (*aut … aut* – either … or)
autem: on top of that; however; moreover
bene: well
beneficium, -iī n.: favor, benefit, kindness; (beneficiō + *gen.*) because of
bēstia, -ae f.: beast
bonus, -a, -um: good, kind(ly), useful
caelum, -ī n.: sky; heaven
calcō (1): trample, tread, step on
cānus, -a, -um: white, gray; gray haired; aged
caput, capitis n.: head; topmost part
carcer, carceris m.: prison
carō, carnis f.: flesh

catēchūmenus, -ī m.: catechumen, a Christian who has not yet been baptized

causa, -ae f.: reason, cause; case

cēterus, -a, -um: the remaining, rest, others

Chrīstus, -ī m.: Christ, the Anointed One

coepī, coepisse, coeptum: to begin

cognōscō, -ere, -gnōvī, -gnitum: to learn, recognize, come to know, *perf.* know

cōnscrībō, -ere, -scrīpsī, -scrīptum: to write down

corpus, corporis n.: body

crēdō, -ere, crēdidī, crēditum: to believe, trust

cum: with (*prep.* + *abl.*)

cum: when, since, although (*conj.*)

cūr: why?

dē: (down) from; about, concerning (+ *abl.*)

dēiciō, -ere, -iēcī, -iectum: to throw down; dissuade

Deus, -ī m.: God

dīcō, -ere, dīxī, dictum: to say, speak, tell, call, name

diēs, -ēī m./f.: day

Dīnocratēs, -is m.: Dinocrates, Perpetua's brother (*acc.* Dīnocratēn)

dō, dare, dedī, datum: to give; grant

doleō, -ēre, doluī, dolitum: to grieve, feel pain, be saddened; to cause pain

dolor, -ōris m.: pain, grief; labor pain

dominus, -ī m.: master, lord

dūcō, -ere, dūxī, ductum: to lead

ē, ex: out from, from, out of (+ *abl.*)

ego, meī, mihi, mē, mē: I, me

enim: for, indeed, in truth

eō, īre, iī, itum: to go

et: and; also; even

exeō, -īre, -iī (-īvī), -itum: to go out; depart; die

expergīscor, expergīscī, experrēctus sum: to wake up, awake

faciēs, -ēī f.: face; expression

faciō, -ere, fēcī, factum: to do, make, perform; grant

Fēlicitās, -tātis f.: Felicity (an enslaved catechumen arrested with Perpetua)

fēmina, -ae f.: a woman

fidēs, -eī f.: faith, belief

fīlia, -ae f.: daughter

fīlius, -iī m.: son; child

fīō, fierī, factus sum: to become; be made; happen

fortis, -e: strong; brave

frāter, -tris m.: brother

gaudeō, -ēre, gāvīsus sum: to enjoy, rejoice

gladius, -ī m.: sword

glōria, -ae f.: glory, fame, praise

grātia, -ae f.: grace; favor; gratitude, thanks
habeō, -ēre, -uī, -itum: to have, hold; consider
hic, haec, hoc: this, these
Hilariānus, -ī m.: Hilarianus (procurator in charge of Perpetua's trial)
hilaris, -e: cheerful, joyous
homō, -inis m.: person, human
iam: now, already, soon
ibi: there, in that place
īdem, eadem, idem: the same (person or thing)
ideō: therefore, for this reason
Iēsus, Iēsū, Iēsū, Iēsum, Iēsū m.: Jesus
ille, illa, illud: that, those
immēnsus, -a, -um: huge, vast, immense
in: in, on; into, to (+ *acc.* or +*abl.*)
īnfāns, īnfantis m./f.: infant, child
inquam: to say, speak (inquit 3rd/sg./pres.)
īnsignis, -e: distinguished; extraordinary
intellegō, -ere, -lēxī, -lēctum: to realize, understand
inter: between, among (+ *acc.*)
introeō, -īre, -īvī (iī), itum: to enter, go into
invicem: in turn; one another
ipse, ipsa, ipsum: himself/herself/itself; the very (person or thing)
is, ea, id: this, that; he, she, it
iste, -a, -ud: this, that
ita: so, thus, in such a way
itaque: and so, therefore; then
leopardus, -ī m.: leopard
locus, -ī m.: place, region, location (neuter in the plural)
magnus, -a, -um: great, large; important
mālō, mālle, māluī: to prefer
mamma, -ae f.: breast
manus, -ūs f.: hand; group
margo, marginis m./f.: border, edge, rim
martyr, martyris m./f.: witness, martyr
māter, mātris f.: mother
medius, -a, -um: in the middle of
meus, -a, -um: my, mine
mīles, mīlitis m.: soldier
mittō, -ere, mīsī, missum: to send; dismiss; throw
modo: only, just now (*adv.*)
modus, -ī m.: way, manner; measure
morior, morī, mortuus sum: to die
multum: greatly, repeatedly (*adv.*)

multus, -a, -um: much; many

mūnus, -eris n.: duty, gift; spectacle, gladiatorial games

nē: lest, that not, no, not

neque: and not, nor

nisi: if not, unless, except

nōlō, nōlle, nōluī: to refuse, be unwilling

nōmen, nōminis n.: name

nōn: not, by no means, not at all

nōs, nostrī/nostrum (gen.), nōbīs, nōs, nōbīs: we, us

noster, nostra, nostrum: our

novus, -a, -um: new, fresh; young; recent, last

nunc: now, at present

ō: o, oh

omnis, -e: every, all

ōrātiō, -tiōnis f.: speech, speaking; prayer

ostendō, -ere, ostendī, ostēnsum: to show

passiō, passiōnis f.: passion, suffering, endurance

pater, patris m.: father

patior, patī, passus sum: to suffer, endure; allow

paucī, -ae, -a: few

per: through, across (+ *acc.*)

Perpetua, -ae f.: Perpetua

perveniō, -īre, -vēnī, -ventum: to arrive

pēs, pedis m.: foot

petō, petere, petīvī, petītum: to seek; request; pray

populus, -ī m.: people, nation; crowd

porta, -ae f.: door, gate

possum, posse, potuī: be able, can

post: after, behind (*prep.* + *acc.*)

post: afterward, next (*adv.*)

postulō (1): to demand, claim, request, ask

prior, prius: earlier, before, previous

prō: before, for, on behalf of, in accordance with (+ *abl.*)

propter: on account of, because of (+ *acc.*)

puella, puellae f.: girl

puer, puerī m.: boy

pugnō (1): to fight

quam: than (comparative + quam)

quam: how ...! what a ...! (in exclamations)

quasi: as it were, so to speak, as if, just as, almost

quattuor: four

-que: and (*enclitic*)

quī, quae, quod: who, which, that

81

quia: because, since

quīdam, quaedam, quiddam: a certain (person or thing)

quisque, quaeque, quodque: each (person or thing)

quod: because (causal conjunction)

quod: when (temporal conjunction)

quōmodo: how, in what way; just as

refrīgerō (1): to cool; to refresh oneself, to be refreshed; to comfort oneself, be comforted

relinquō, -ere, -līquī, -lictum: to leave behind; abandon

rēs, reī f.: thing; matter; affair; business

respondeō, -ēre, -dī, -ōnsum: to respond, answer

saeculum, -ī n.: age; generation; this present world

salvus, -a, -um: safe, unharmed

sānctus, -a, -um: sacred, holy

sanguis, -inis m.: blood

Satūrus, -ī m.: Satyrus (teacher of the catechumens)

scāla, -ae f.: ladder; flight of stairs

sciō, -īre, -īvī (iī), -ītum: to know (how)

sē: himself, herself, itself, themselves

secundus, -a, -um: following, favorable; second

sed: but

semper: always, forever

senex, senis m.: old, old man

sī: if

sīc: thus, in this way

sine: without (+ *abl.*)

soror, sorōris f.: sister

spatium, -iī n.: space, room, extent

spēs, speī f.: hope; expectation

spīritus, -ūs m.: spirit

statim: immediately, at once

stō, -āre, stetī, statum: to stand, set; to stand firm

sub: under, below, beneath (+ *acc.* or +*abl.*)

sum, esse, fuī, futūrum: to be

super: above; over, on

suus, -a, -um: his, her, its, their own

tālis, -e: such, of such a kind

tamen: however, nevertheless

tantum: only (*adv.*)

tantus, -a, -um: so great, so large, such

terra, -ae f.: earth, ground, land

tū, tuī, tibi, tē, tē: you

tunc: then, at that time

tuus, -a, -um: your, yours

ubi: where, when

ūniversus, -a, -um: entire; all, all together

ūnus, -a, -um: one

ursus, -ī m.: bear

ūsque: all the way to, up to (+ *acc.*)

ūsque: continuously (*adv.*)

ut: as, just as, like; when, because (+ *indicative.*); (so) that, in order that (+ *subjunctive*)

utique: in any case, at any rate, at least

vel: or, either ... or; even

veniō, -īre, vēnī, ventum: come, go

verbum, -ī n.: word, speech

vetus, -eris: old, experienced, ancient

via, -ae f.: road, way, path

videō, vidēre, vīdī, vīsum: to see; (in passive) to seem

vir, virī m.: man

virtūs, -tūtis f.: excellence, virtue; courage, power; an act of courage

vīsiō, -ōnis f.: vision, apparition

vocō (1): call, name, address, summon

volō, velle, voluī: will, wish, be willing

vōs, vestrī/vestrum, vōbīs, vōs, vōbīs: you (plural)